What People Are Saying about Threshold Bible Study

"Besides furnishing the reader with solid biblical analysis, this remarkable series provides a method of study and reflection, for both individuals and groups, that is bound to produce rich fruit. This well developed thematic approach to Bible study is meant to wed serious study and personal prayer within a reflective context. Stephen Binz is to be applauded for this fine addition to Bible study programs."

Dianne Bergant, C.S.A., professor of Old Testament,
Catholic Theological Union, Chicago

"The Threshold Bible Study connects the wisdom of God's Word to our daily lives. This fine series will provide needed tools that can deepen your understanding of Scripture, but most importantly it can deepen your faith. In the classical tradition of lectio divina, this series also offers a very practical way to pray with Scripture, and I can think of nothing better for equipping people for the New Evangelization than a biblically soaked life of prayer."

Most Reverend Charles J. Chaput, O.F.M. Cap., Archbishop of Denver

"Here, at last, is a Bible study for those of us who don't like Bible studies! Rather than focusing on a book, Stephen Binz invites us to view many well-known passages through the lens of a particular theme, bringing new meaning to the passages and deeper connection to the theme in our own lives. His discussions do far more than inform; they ask for commitment and assent on the part of the reader/prayer."

Kathleen O'Connell Chesto, author or F.I.R.E. and *Why Are the Dandelions Weeds?*

"Threshold Bible Study offers a marvelous new approach for individuals and groups to study themes in our rich biblical and theological tradition. Moving through these thematic units feels like gazing at panels of stained glass windows, viewing similar images through different lights."

John Endres, S.J., professor of Scripture, Jesuit School of Theology, Berkeley

"The Church has called Scripture a 'font' and 'wellspring' for the spiritual life. Threshold Bible Study is one of the best sources for tapping into the biblical font. Pope John Paul II has stressed that 'listening to the Word of God should become a life-giving encounter.' This is precisely what Threshold Bible Study offers to you—an encounter with the Word that will make your heart come alive."

Tim Gray, Director of the Denver Catholic Biblical School

PILGRIMAGE *in the* FOOTSTEPS *of* JESUS

Stephen J. Binz

TWENTY
THIRD 23rd
PUBLICATIONS

All photographs within are the work of the author ©Stephen J. Binz.

The content and format of this study has been adapted from material previously published in *God's Word Today* magazine. The founding editor is George Martin and the present editor is Jean-Pierre Prévost.

The Scripture passages contained herein are from the *New Revised Standard Version of the Bible*, Catholic edition. Copyright © 1989, by the Division of Christian Education of the National Council of Churches in the U.S.A. All rights reserved.

Second printing 2006

Twenty-Third Publications
A Division of Bayard
One Montauk Avenue, Suite 200
New London, CT 06320
(860) 437-3012 or (800) 321-0411
www.twentythirdpublications.com

ISBN-10: 1-58595-318-0
ISBN-13: 978-1-58595-318-9
Library of Congress: 2003113285
Printed in the U.S.A.

Contents

LESSONS 13-18

LESSONS 19-24

LESSONS 25-30

How to Use
Threshold Bible Study

Each book in the Threshold Bible Study series is designed to lead you through a new doorway of biblical awareness, to accompany you across a new threshold of understanding. The characters, places, and images that you will encounter in each of these topical studies will help you explore new dimensions of your faith and discover deeper insights for your spiritual life.

Threshold Bible Study covers biblical themes in depth in a short amount of time. Unlike more traditional Bible studies that treat a biblical book or series of books, Threshold Bible Study is designed to address specific topics within the entire Bible. The goal is not for you to comprehend everything about each passage, but rather for you to understand what a variety of passages from different books of the Bible reveals about the topic of each study.

Threshold Bible Study offers you an opportunity to explore the entire Bible from the point of view of a variety of different themes. The commentary that follows each biblical passage launches your reflection about that passage and helps you begin to see the significance of the passage in the context of your contemporary experience. The questions following the commentary challenge you to understand the passage more clearly and apply it to your own life. The prayer starter helps you conclude your study by integrating your learning into your relationship with God.

These studies are designed for maximum flexibility. Their format encourages their use both for individual study and group discussion. They are ideal for Bible study groups, small Christian communities, student groups, Sunday school, neighborhood groups, and family reading, as well as for individual learning. Each study is presented in a workbook format, designed for reading, reflecting, writing, discussing, and praying. Space for writing after each question is ideal for personal study and allows group members to prepare in advance for the discussion. The thirty lessons in each study may be used by an individual for daily study over the period of a month, or they may be divided into six lessons per week, providing a group study of six weekly sessions.

The method of Threshold Bible Study is rooted in the classical tradition of "lectio divina," an ancient yet contemporary means for reading the Scriptures reflectively and prayerfully. Reading and interpreting the text (*lectio*) is followed by reflective meditation on its message (*meditatio*). This reading and reflecting flows into prayer from the heart (*oratio* and *contemplatio*).

This ancient method assures us that Bible study is a matter of both the mind and the heart. It is not just an intellectual exercise to learn more and be able to discuss the Bible with others. It is, more importantly, a transforming experience. Reflecting on God's word, guided by the Holy Spirit, illumines the mind with wisdom and stirs the heart with zeal.

Following the personal Bible study, Threshold Bible Study offers a method for extending "lectio divina" into a weekly conversation with a small group. This communal experience will allow participants to enhance their appreciation of the message and build up a spiritual community (*collatio*). The end result will be to increase not only individual faith, but also faithful witness in the context of daily life. Both the individual and group experience will lead participants to actualize the word and live it in the world (*operatio*).

Through the spiritual disciplines of Scripture reading, study, reflection, conversation, and prayer, you will experience God's grace more abundantly and deepen your life in Christ. The risen Jesus said: "Listen! I am standing at the door, knocking; if you hear my voice and open the door, I will come in to you and eat with you, and you with me" (Rev 3:20). Listen to the Word of God, open the door, and cross the threshold to a more abundant dwelling with God!

SUGGESTIONS FOR INDIVIDUAL STUDY

• Make your Bible reading a time of prayer. Ask for God's guidance as you read the Scriptures.

• Try to do your study daily, or as often as possible in the circumstances of your life.

• Read the Bible passage carefully, trying to understand both its meaning and its personal application as you read. Some find it helpful to read the passage aloud.

• Read the passage in another Bible translation. Each version adds to your understanding of the original text.

• Allow the commentary to help you comprehend and apply the scriptural text. The commentary is only a beginning to understanding, not the last word on the meaning of the passage.

• After reflecting on each question, write out your responses. The very act of writing will help you clarify your thoughts, bring you new insights, and amplify your understanding.

• As you reflect on your answers, think about how to actualize God's word and live it in the context of your daily life.

• Conclude each daily lesson by reading the prayer and continuing with your own prayer from the heart.

• Make sure your reflections and prayers are matters of both the mind and the heart. An encounter with God's word is always a transforming experience.

• Choose a word or a phrase from the lesson to carry with you throughout the day as a reminder of your encounter with God's life-changing word.

• Share what you are learning with at least one other person whom you trust for additional insights and affirmation. The ideal way to share learning is in a small group that meets regularly.

SUGGESTIONS FOR GROUP STUDY

• Meet regularly; weekly is ideal. Try to be on time and make attendance a high priority for the sake of the group. The average group meets for about an hour.

• Open each session with a prepared prayer, a song, or a reflection. Find some appropriate way of bringing the group from the workaday world into a sacred time of graced sharing.

• Get acquainted with the other group members, if you have not been together before. Name tags can be helpful as a group begins to meet.

• Spend the first session getting acquainted with one another, reading the Introduction to the study aloud, and discussing the questions.

• Appoint a group facilitator to provide guidance to the discussion. The role of facilitator may rotate among members each week. The facilitator simply keeps the discussion on track; each person shares responsibility for the group. There is no need for the facilitator to be a trained teacher.

• Try to study the six lessons on your own during the week. When you have done your own reflection and written your own answers, you will be better prepared to discuss the six scriptural lessons with the group each week. If you have not had an opportunity to study the passages during the week, meet with the group anyway to share support and insights.

• Participate in the discussion as much as you are able, offering your thoughts, insights, feelings, and decisions. Plan to share what God has taught you during your individual study. You learn by participating and you offer to others the fruits of your study.

• Be careful not to dominate the discussion. It is important that all in the group be offered an equal opportunity to share the results of their work. Try to link what you say to the comments of others so that the group remains on the topic.

• When discussing your own personal thoughts or feelings, try to use "I" language. Be as personal and honest as possible when appropriate and be very cautious about giving advice to others.

• Listen attentively to the other members of the group. Expect that you will learn from the insights of others. The words of the Bible affect each person in a different way, so a group provides a wealth of understanding for each member.

• Don't fear silence. Silence in a group is as important as silence in personal study. It allows time for members to listen to the voice of God's Spirit and gives them an opportunity to form their thoughts before they speak.

• Solicit several responses for each question. The thoughts of different people will build on the answers of others and will lead to deeper insights for all.

• Don't fear controversy. Differences of opinions are a sign of a healthy and honest group. If you cannot resolve an issue, go on, agreeing to disagree. There is probably some truth in each viewpoint.

• Discuss the questions that seem most important for the group. There is no need to cover all the questions in the group session.

• Realize that some questions about the Bible are irresolvable, even by experts. Don't get stuck on some issue for which there are no clear answers.

• Pray as a group in whatever way feels comfortable. Pray for the members of your group throughout the week.

Schedule for group study

Session 1: Introduction   Date _____

Session 2: Lessons 1-6   Date _____

Session 3: Lessons 7-12   Date _____

Session 4: Lessons 13-18   Date _____

Session 5: Lessons 19-24   Date _____

Session 6: Lessons 25-30   Date _____

Pilgrimage is an attitude.
Attitude —

Pilgrimage is a memory.
Memory —

Christian Life as a pilgrimage.

A place where I encounter God...
It has been different places & things
throughout my life.

① "We belong to the Land"
② "Blood Brothers"
       Father Shakur
Bishop of Galilee

3 Churches   Armenian, Greek Orthodox,
  - Nativity   Roman Catholics
  - Holy Sepulcre
  - Our Father   Jewish | Muslim
                       Armenian | Christian

**As they were going along the road, someone said to Jesus,
"I will follow you wherever you go."** Luke 9:57

Pilgrimage in the Footsteps of Jesus

A pilgrim is someone who goes on a journey in the hope of encountering God, or of meeting God in a new way. There are many sacred places throughout the world frequented by pilgrims seeking to draw closer to God. But for the Christian, the Holy Land is unique. Christians travel to the Holy Land, not because God is present there in a way in which he is not in New York, Paris, or Shanghai. We go there because it is the place where our faith has its deepest roots. Here are the places where Jesus himself walked and talked, laughed and wept, where he was born, lived, suffered, died, and rose again. These places hold a memory of Jesus that carries an enormous sense of expectation for one seeking a fresh encounter with God.

Some have described the Holy Land as the fifth gospel. There are four sacred texts, but there is also the good news about Jesus revealed to us by the places which mark the events of his life. The gospel of the land can fill out the written gospels with tangible reality. Here we can imagine Jesus with his disciples along the lake, teaching on the mountainside, praying in the garden, and dying on the cross. In this fifth gospel we realize that we have inherited not only a history of salvation, but a geography of salvation. God was revealed to us in Jesus Christ not only in a specific period of history, but also in very specific places. Through studying the geography of God's revelation in Jesus, we come to realize how truly incarnational is our Christian faith.

Reflection and discussion

• Considering the above definition of pilgrimage, have I ever taken a pilgrimage, either internally or externally?

• How could studying the places of Jesus' life help me better understand the incarnational reality of my Christian faith (John 1:14)?

The Bible is filled with the stories of people traveling on pilgrimage. Abraham and Sarah left their homeland to journey to a new land which God would show them. They went out not knowing where they were going, traveling by faith at God's direction. Moses led the Hebrews from slavery to the land God had promised. They encountered God on that long journey and became God's people through the experience. The life of Jesus too was essentially an earthly pilgrimage, the goal of which was his return to the Father. He shows us the way to follow in his footsteps as we journey through life along our pilgrim way.

Christian pilgrims from the early centuries of the church traveled to the land in which Jesus himself was a pilgrim. They had their Bibles in hand, and they wanted to touch the places of his life which they had read about in the Scriptures. By the fourth century, Constantine, the first Christian emperor of Rome, began encouraging pilgrimage to the holy places of the faith after the pilgrimage of his mother, St. Helen.

Constantine built three major basilicas in the Holy Land, each built around a cave associated with the life of Jesus. He constructed the Church of the Resurrection which included a circular shrine at the empty tomb of Christ as well as a memorial at the site of Calvary. Constantine also erected the Eleona Church on the Mount of Olives, built around a cave honoring the place where Jesus frequently taught his disciples. The third basilica was the Church of the

Nativity in Bethlehem, focused on the cave marking the place of Jesus' birth.

While Constantine's churches were being built, an anonymous pilgrim from Bordeaux came to follow in the footsteps of Jesus. From him we have the first writings describing a tour through the Holy Land. He carefully noted routes and distances, and his descriptions of places like Golgotha, the house of Caiaphas, and the tomb of Lazarus confirm the antiquity of many traditions about the holy places. St. Jerome, a fourth-century biblical scholar who traveled the land, wrote this: "We will have a clearer grasp of Scripture after we have gazed with our own eyes on the sites where the events of our salvation unfolded."

The most extensive early travelogue was written by a woman named Egeria. Her writings describe the fourth-century rituals of Holy Week in Jerusalem. She described the Palm Sunday procession from the Mount of Olives, the Holy Thursday liturgy which ended by walking to Gethsemane by torchlight, and the Good Friday veneration of the cross. She then describes the Paschal Vigil at the Church of the Resurrection with its baptisms and Eucharist.

A beloved pilgrim of the Middle Ages was St. Francis of Assisi. In 1219 he journeyed to bring the message of peace to the Crusaders and the Muslim forces who were battling over the Holy Land. He encouraged his followers to travel to the land where Jesus lived. From that time on the Franciscans have staffed many of the places associated with the life of Jesus.

From these early pilgrims we realize that the holy places marking events in the life of Jesus are preserved not just for people to view. Many of them have been made into shrines or churches for liturgical worship. Through worship, the saving event is evoked and becomes sacramentally present for the worshiper. In liturgy the past becomes present; God acts in the lives of the pilgrims just as surely as God acted in the lives of those first followers of Jesus. Pilgrimage is more than a journey which recalls the past; it is a sacramental action, an experience that makes the sacred past present again.

The gospel account of the journey along the road to Emmaus (Luke 24:13–35) describes some of the most important aspects of Christian pilgrimage. The travelers along the way encounter Jesus who accompanies them on their journey. They discuss their life experiences along the way and they read from the Scriptures. The travelers offer hospitality and they break bread together. The journey became a pilgrimage because they experienced the Risen Lord. He was present with them on the road, in the words exchanged, in the Scriptures, in the signs of hospitality, in the Eucharist, and in the community formed through the experience. The experience of Christ in the journey offered new possibilities and new hope for their pilgrim lives. These are the elements of pilgrimage: journey, community, Scripture, sacrifice, hospitality, ritual, sacrament, and spiritual encounter.

Reflection and discussion

• What favorite memories do I make present again through celebration and ritual?

• In what ways could I describe my Christian life as a pilgrimage?

• Has a particular place ever been a means for me to encounter God?

The value of pilgrimage to sacred places has always been debatable for Christians, in the same way that venerating sacred images has been contentious. Religious images were destroyed during the eighth and ninth century iconoclast controversy because it was thought that divinity should not be expressed in material forms. Similarly, pilgrimage was sometimes discouraged because it was thought that earthly places and human structures could get in the way of spiritual encounters with God. Had not Jesus said to the Samaritan woman that true worship had nothing to do with Jerusalem or Samaria, but was all about worshipping God in spirit and in truth (John

4:20–24)? We are too easily tempted to believe that going to a particular place or going through a particular ritual earns us God's favor.

Yet images, places, and rituals can indeed be powerful means to experience God. God is at work in creation. Because God has become incarnate in the world, we can discover the presence of God through the world, especially through those created people, places, and things that remind us of God. All the world is holy and has a sacramental quality, speaking to us of the goodness of God. Particularly the places where Jesus spent his earthly life can be effective signs of his presence and love, effective means of his grace.

When controversies arose about the value of pilgrimage, Jerome said that external pilgrimage must always be accompanied by interior conversion. "It is not sufficient merely to go on pilgrimage," he said. "Its success depends upon the pilgrim's ability to journey in faith, with a new heart and with a will to conversion. Otherwise the journey might be the same as any other." Pilgrimage is the simultaneous movement of the feet and the soul.

The ambiguity of Christian pilgrimage to holy places is summed up by the words of the angel at the empty tomb: "Come, see the place," is balanced by "He is not here, he has been raised" (Matt 28:6). Because Jesus is the Risen Lord, the empty tomb at the Church of the Holy Sepulcher is not necessarily any holier than my own living room. The whole world has become the Holy Land. The value of pilgrimage is determined by the persons we have become when we come back home. Pilgrimage to holy places can be for many an experience of real growth in discipleship, but the deepest value of pilgrimage is found in returning home and realizing that God was waiting for us there all the while. Sometimes it is necessary to go halfway around the world to discover that all the answers are within us.

Ultimately it is not we who travel looking for God. It is really God who is looking for us. When we go on pilgrimage humbly, listening for God to speak in the silence of our hearts, waiting for God to show us his presence, there is no telling in what ways we may be changed.

As we reflect on the sacred places and Scriptures contained in this Bible study, we will unite our hearts with pilgrims through the ages and become pilgrims ourselves. Through the living word of God, the risen Lord is present with us, walking along our pilgrim way. As pilgrims our understanding of the gospels will be enriched through this study as we form connections between the sacred text and the holy places.

Reflection and discussion

• How could a greater understand of geography and topography fill out my understanding of the gospels?

• What is the difference between a tourist and a pilgrim?

• What do I expect to be different after I complete my study of the places of Jesus' life?

Many Christians desire someday to take a pilgrimage to the Holy Land, but as in many periods of history, the costs and dangers of travel to the Middle East, as well as work and family responsibilities, make such a trip prohibitive for now. Hopefully this study of the places of Jesus' life on earth will provide a real pilgrimage experience for homebound and workbound pilgrims. This pilgrimage in the footsteps of Jesus will be a personal and spiritual pilgrimage to the holy ground of the life of Jesus.

Prayer

Word made flesh, you have come and pitched your tent in our world. In your unfathomable will, you have come to us in a particular location in our world, through the ancient faith of Judaism, in a particular era of history. You had unique personal features and a distinct personality, you grew up in a human family, and you traveled to particular places. You have truly become incarnate in our humanity. Be present to us with your Holy Spirit as we study the places of your earthly life so that we can come to know you more personally. Guide us on our pilgrimage together.

SUGGESTIONS FOR FACILITATORS, GROUP SESSION 1

1. If the group is meeting for the first time, or if there are newcomers joining the group, it is helpful to provide nametags.

2. Distribute the books to the members of the group.

3. You may want to ask the participants to introduce themselves and tell the group a bit about themselves.

4. Ask one or more of these introductory questions:
• What attracted you to this study on pilgrimage?
• How is beginning this study like a "threshold" for you?

5. You may want to pray this prayer as a group:
Come upon us, Holy Spirit, to enlighten and guide us as we begin this pilgrimage in the footsteps of Jesus. As we explore the places in the Holy Land today that mark the places in the life of Jesus, give us the spiritual gift of imagination. May the mountains and water, the cities and villages, the ruins and shrines of our pilgrimage fill our memories and be means to experience your grace. Accompany us on our journey and guide our way. Motivate us to read the Scriptures, give us a love for God's word, and help us to know Jesus more personally and more richly. Bless us during this session and throughout the coming week with the fire of your love.

6. Read the Introduction aloud, pausing at each question for discussion. Group members may wish to write the insights of the group as each question is discussed. Encourage several members of the group to respond to each question.

7. Don't feel compelled to finish the complete Introduction during the session. It is better to allow sufficient time to talk about the questions raised than to rush to the end. Group members may read any remaining sections on their own after the group meeting.

8. Instruct group members to read the first six lessons on their own before the next group meeting. They should write out their own answers to the questions as preparation for next week's group discussion.

9. Conclude by praying aloud together the prayer at the end of the Introduction.

**The angel Gabriel was sent by God to a town
in Galilee called Nazareth.** Luke 1:26

Nazareth: Basilica of the Annunciation

LUKE 1:26–38 ²⁶*In the sixth month the angel Gabriel was sent by God to a town in Galilee called Nazareth,* ²⁷*to a virgin engaged to a man whose name was Joseph, of the house of David. The virgin's name was Mary.* ²⁸*And he came to her and said, "Greetings, favored one! The Lord is with you."* ²⁹*But she was much perplexed by his words and pondered what sort of greeting this might be.* ³⁰*The angel said to her, "Do not be afraid, Mary, for you have found favor with God.* ³¹*And now, you will conceive in your womb and bear a son, and you will name him Jesus.* ³²*He will be great, and will be called the Son of the Most High, and the Lord God will give to him the throne of his ancestor David.* ³³*He will reign over the house of Jacob forever, and of his kingdom there will be no end."* ³⁴*Mary said to the angel, "How can this be, since I am a virgin?"* ³⁵*The angel said to her, "The Holy Spirit will come upon you, and the power of the Most High will overshadow you; therefore the child to be born will be holy; he will be called Son of God.* ³⁶*And now, your relative Elizabeth in her old age has also conceived a son; and this is the sixth month for her who was said to be barren.* ³⁷*For nothing will be impossible with God."* ³⁸*Then Mary said, "Here am I, the servant of the Lord; let it be with me according to your word." Then the angel departed from her.*

Nazareth, still a small town situated in the hills of Galilee, is the place where the life of Jesus began. Today Nazareth is dominated by the Basilica of the Annunciation. On the lower level of the church, directly beneath the starlike lantern within the dome, are the remains of a natural cave.

A very ancient and reliable tradition points to this place as the house of Mary, where Gabriel revealed her central role in God's saving plan. Early pilgrims left their markings—called "graffiti" by archaeologists—on the cave walls. Among the graffiti are the letters XE MARIA, "Hail Mary," the oldest known inscription honoring Mary. A shrine was built on this site in the third century and at least four churches have enclosed this site through the centuries: Byzantine, Crusader, eighteenth-century Franciscan, and the present basilica. The present site incorporates the remains from each of these periods.

Throughout the world church bells ring as Christians pray the Angelus: "The angel of the Lord declared unto Mary; and she conceived by the Holy Spirit. I am the handmaid of the Lord; let it be done to me according to your word. The word was made flesh and dwelt among us." At the altar of the Annunciation the words are inscribed: Verbum Caro Hic Factum Est (Here the Word was made flesh). Every March 25, nine months before the celebration of Jesus' birth, the church throughout the world celebrates the feast of the Annunciation.

The double emphasis that Mary is a virgin (verse 27) indicates the total newness of this new creation of God. "The Lord is with you" (verse 28) and "Do not be afraid" (verse 30) are God's frequent pledges of divine guidance and protection throughout the Old Testament. The angel announced that the child to be born would be the promised Messiah (verses 32–33) and the Son of God (verse 35). Through his conception in the womb of Mary, Jesus would have an unparalleled relationship with the God of Israel. "The Most High," "the Son of God," and "the Holy Spirit" are present to Mary at this climactic moment of saving grace (verse 35).

To this day, the people of the Middle East make a bow with the hand placed against the chest as an indication that one is willing to obey another's wish. Mary bowed before God: "Let it be with me according to your word" (verse 38). She has willed that God possess her life and she knows that will influence everything that happens in her life from now on.

Reflection and discussion

• Why is this basilica the best place to begin a pilgrimage through the life of Jesus?

• In what ways is Mary a model of trust for me?

• What gives me confidence in God's plan for me? Do I respond to God with hope?

• What would it mean for me to say to God, "Let it be with me according to your word"?

Prayer

Son of Mary, help me see the holiness of my home and work, and give me a heart that is open to your word. Teach me to respond to the Father's plan for me with simple trust and the obedience of love.

"Joseph, son of David, do not be afraid to take Mary as your wife, for the child conceived in her is from the Holy Spirit." Matt 1:20

Nazareth: Church of St. Joseph

MATTHEW 1:18–25 [18]*Now the birth of Jesus the Messiah took place in this way. When his mother Mary had been engaged to Joseph, but before they lived together, she was found to be with child from the Holy Spirit.* [19]*Her husband Joseph, being a righteous man and unwilling to expose her to public disgrace, planned to dismiss her quietly.* [20]*But just when he had resolved to do this, an angel of the Lord appeared to him in a dream and said, "Joseph, son of David, do not be afraid to take Mary as your wife, for the child conceived in her is from the Holy Spirit.* [21]*She will bear a son, and you are to name him Jesus, for he will save his people from their sins."* [22]*All this took place to fulfill what had been spoken by the Lord through the prophet:* [23]*"Look, the virgin shall conceive and bear a son, and they shall name him Emmanuel" which means, "God is with us."* [24]*When Joseph awoke from sleep, he did as the angel of the Lord commanded him; he took her as his wife,* [25]*but had no marital relations with her until she had borne a son; and he named him Jesus.*

MATTHEW 2:19–23 [19]*When Herod died, an angel of the Lord suddenly appeared in a dream to Joseph in Egypt and said,* [20]*"Get up, take the child and his mother, and go to the land of Israel, for those who were seeking the child's life* *are dead." ²¹Then Joseph got up, took the child and his mother, and went to the land of Israel. ²²But when he heard that Archelaus was ruling over Judea in place of his father Herod, he was afraid to go there. And after being warned in a dream, he went away to the district of Galilee. ²³There he made his home in a town called Nazareth, so that what had been spoken through the prophets might be fulfilled, "He will be called a Nazorean."*

Near the Basilica of the Annunciation is the Church of St. Joseph, commemorating the house and workshop of Joseph. Here is remembered the annunciation to Joseph. Mary and Joseph were betrothed; they had formally exchanged their consent and their marriage was legally contracted. The second stage of their Jewish marriage would come later as the bride would be festively transferred to the house of the groom. Discovering the pregnancy of Mary, this "righteous man" did not want to expose her to public humiliation and had decided to give her the prescribed document of divorce privately. But his agonizing choice was cut short by the revelation of God's plan in a dream.

Through Joseph's compliant response to God's will, Jesus is able to be called Son of David, and thus Messiah of Israel (1:20). Through the working of the Holy Spirit in Mary, Jesus is able to be called the Son of God. The complementary and obedient responses of both Mary and Joseph are necessary for the coming of the Savior.

The Church of St. Joseph also commemorates the place where Jesus grew up. Excavations under the church have revealed a series of cisterns for holding water and granaries which stored the fruit of the fertile fields surrounding Nazareth. This was the heart of the town in the days of Jesus. Matthew 13:55 refers to Jesus as the son of a tekton, and Mark 6:3 calls Jesus a *tekton* (usually translated "carpenter"). This Greek word means "craftsman," one who works in stone, metal, or wood. Joseph was not a carpenter in our limited sense of the word, but was a skilled craftsman who built houses, made agricultural tools, and repaired almost anything. Joseph taught his son both the faith of Judaism and the skills of his trade.

Jesus would be known as a "Nazorean" (2:23). Beneath the cars and buses, houses and hotels of today, lies the Jewish peasant village. In modern Nazareth we can still observe many characteristics of an ancient oriental town. The *souk*, or marketplace, displays fruits and vegetables, live chickens and fresh meat, woven cloths and jewelry. In the shop owners of the town we can still see people like Joseph and Mary, with their olive skin and deep-set eyes.

We can see Jesus in the children as they run through the streets and out into the hills overlooking the great valley below. We see Jesus in the youth who help the elders of the town in their shops and learn new skills from their parents. Jesus is in the young men who go to the churches for the feasts as Jesus went to the synagogue on Saturdays and learned the Scriptures. This small town, belittled as an insignificant place by the religious leaders of Jerusalem (John 1:46), was the hometown of the one who would save his people (1:21).

Reflection and discussion

• Why would God come among us in such humble and human ways?

• Have I ever received a message from God through a dream? In what other ways do I discern God's will?

• What does Joseph teach me about the value of my work and family life?

Prayer

Son of David and Son of Joseph, you came among us to be Emmanuel—God with us. Show me that you are present and close to me in my work, my play, as well as my prayer. Teach me how to make my home a sacred dwelling for you.

Mary set out and went with haste to a Judean town in the hill country, where she entered the house of Zechariah and greeted Elizabeth. Luke 1:39–40

Ein Karem: Church of the Visitation

LUKE 1:39–56 ³⁹*In those days Mary set out and went with haste to a Judean town in the hill country, ⁴⁰where she entered the house of Zechariah and greeted Elizabeth. ⁴¹When Elizabeth heard Mary's greeting, the child leaped in her womb. And Elizabeth was filled with the Holy Spirit ⁴²and exclaimed with a loud cry, "Blessed are you among women, and blessed is the fruit of your womb. And why has this happened to me, that the mother of my Lord comes to me? ⁴⁴For as soon as I heard the sound of your greeting, the child in my womb leaped for joy. And blessed is she who believed that there would be a fulfillment of what was spoken to her by the Lord."*

⁴⁶*Mary said,*

"My soul magnifies the Lord,

⁴⁷*and my spirit rejoices in God my Savior,*

⁴⁸*for he has looked with favor on the lowliness of his servant.*

Surely, from now on all generations will call me blessed;

⁴⁹*for the Mighty One has done great things for me,*

and holy is his name.

⁵⁰*His mercy is for those who fear him*

from generation to generation.
⁵¹*He has shown strength with his arm;*
  he has scattered the proud in the thoughts of their hearts.
⁵²*He has brought down the powerful from their thrones,*
  and lifted up the lowly;
⁵³*he has filled the hungry with good things,*
  and sent the rich away empty.
⁵⁴*He has helped his servant Israel,*
  in remembrance of his mercy,
⁵⁵*according to the promise he made to our ancestors,*
  to Abraham and to his descendants forever."
  ⁵⁶*And Mary remained with her about three months and then returned to her home.*

A few miles west of Jerusalem, picturesquely set within the folds of Judean hills, is a quiet village named Ein Karem. Its name means "spring of the vineyard." Today that spring still flows as the source of water for the town and irrigation for its crops. Tradition tells us that here in Ein Karem lived Elizabeth and Zechariah, and their child John who would "prepare the way" for Jesus.

High above the village is the Church of the Visitation, commemorating the meeting of Mary and Elizabeth. The mosaic on the façade of the church shows Mary traveling on her way from Nazareth to Elizabeth's home. The frescoes of the lower church show Zachariah as a priest in the Temple of Jerusalem (1:5–23), Elizabeth hiding the infant John from Herod's soldiers (Matt 2:16), and the joyful greeting of Mary and Elizabeth.

Mary had been told by the angel that her elderly relative Elizabeth was to have a child (1:36), and Mary's immediate response was to travel the eighty miles to care for her. The two women represent the old covenant and the new covenant. Elizabeth is elderly and will have a son who will be the last great figure of ancient Israel; Mary is young and will have a son who will usher in the new age of salvation. In Mary the new covenant reaches out to the old covenant, giving it ultimate meaning and preparing for its fulfillment. In Elizabeth the old covenant recognizes the new and gives honor to its coming.

Elizabeth praises Mary as "blessed" for two reasons: first, because she is "mother of the Lord" (verses 42–43), and second, because she is model of faith—"blessed is she who believed that there would be a fulfillment of what was spoken to her by the Lord" (verse 45). We honor Mary most often for the first reason; she is the divinely chosen mother of the Son of God. But for the adult Jesus, the second reason seems even most important. When a woman in the crowd surrounding Jesus cried out, "Blessed is the womb that bore you and the breasts that nursed you," Jesus replied, "Blessed rather are those who hear the word of God and obey it!" (11:27–28). Truly Mary bore the word of God both in her womb and in her heart.

Mary's canticle of praise, the Magnificat, is inscribed on ceramic plaques in a multitude of languages in the peaceful courtyard of the Church of the Visitation. In harmony with the flowers of the Judean hill country that spring day, Mary opened like a rose as her whole being unfolded in song. The musical words of her canticle sent forth the good news of God's salvation down through the ages as blossoms release their scent upon the wind. God is answering his ancient promises, lifting up the lowly and giving hope to all who wait. The mother of the Lord sings and all generations rejoice.

Reflection and discussion

• How is the Spirit working in my life? Revealing how God is at work within me? Urging me to help someone in need? Lifting up my heart in praise?

• For what reasons do I choose to honor Mary?

Prayer

> Lord of the old and the new, help me to see how you have been at work throughout the history of the world and the history of my life. May I, like Mary, praise your greatness and rejoice in your wondrous deeds.

**"You, child, will be called the Prophet of the Most High;
for you will go before the Lord to prepare his ways."** Luke 1:76

Ein Karem: Church of St. John the Baptist

LUKE 1:57–80 *⁵⁷Now the time came for Elizabeth to give birth, and she bore a son. ⁵⁸Her neighbors and relatives heard that the Lord had shown his great mercy to her, and they rejoiced with her.*

⁵⁹On the eighth day they came to circumcise the child, and they were going to name him Zechariah after his father. ⁶⁰But his mother said, "No; he is to be called John." ⁶¹They said to her, "None of your relatives has this name." ⁶²Then they began motioning to his father to find out what name he wanted to give him. ⁶³He asked for a writing tablet and wrote, "His name is John." And all of them were amazed. ⁶⁴Immediately his mouth was opened and his tongue freed, and he began to speak, praising God. ⁶⁵Fear came over all their neighbors, and all these things were talked about throughout the entire hill country of Judea. ⁶⁶All who heard them pondered them and said, "What then will this child become?" For, indeed, the hand of the Lord was with him.

⁶⁷Then his father Zechariah was filled with the Holy Spirit and spoke this prophecy:

⁶⁸"Blessed be the Lord God of Israel,
for he has looked favorably on his people and redeemed them.

⁶⁹*He has raised up a mighty savior for us*
   in the house of his servant David,
⁷⁰*as he spoke through the mouth of his holy prophets from of old,*
   ⁷¹*that we would be saved from our enemies and from the hand of all*
   who hate us.
⁷²*Thus he has shown the mercy promised to our ancestors,*
   and has remembered his holy covenant,
⁷³*the oath that he swore to our ancestor Abraham,*
   to grant us ⁷⁴*that we, being rescued from the hands of our enemies,*
   might serve him without fear, ⁷⁵*in holiness and righteousness*
   before him all our days.
⁷⁶*And you, child, will be called the prophet of the Most High;*
   for you will go before the Lord to prepare his ways,
⁷⁷*to give knowledge of salvation to his people*
   by the forgiveness of their sins.
⁷⁸*By the tender mercy of our God,*
   the dawn from on high will break upon us,
⁷⁹*to give light to those who sit in darkness and in the shadow of death,*
   to guide our feet into the way of peace.”
⁸⁰*The child grew and became strong in spirit, and he was in the wilderness until the day he appeared publicly to Israel.*

The Church of St. John the Baptist, also in the village of Ein Karem, honors the birth of John. To the left of the church's sanctuary is a staircase leading down to the Grotto of the Nativity of St. John. The marble reliefs on its walls illustrate the life of John.

The birth, circumcision, naming, and manifestation of John evoke memories of the Old Testament. Like Abraham and Sarah (Gen 21:1–6), the elderly Zechariah and Elizabeth have a son in fulfillment of God's promises. Like their ancestors, they name their son and circumcise him on the eighth day after his birth. The scene at both births was one of laughter and rejoicing by all who heard the news.

The name John means "Yahweh has shown favor." John came as a divine favor to Elizabeth and he will manifest God's favor upon all Israel. Zechariah named his son according to the command of the angel, reversing his earlier reluctance to believe God's word, a doubt which caused him to become mute

(1:20). Because he opened his heart, God opened his mouth. Zechariah's response now matches that of Mary and Elizabeth. As he obeys God's word, he is freed to give praise to God in song (verses 67–79).

The text of Zechariah's canticle, the Benedictus, written in many languages, adorns the walls of the courtyard outside the church. Zechariah's canticle begins in the traditional Jewish prayer style: "Blessed be the Lord God of Israel." It is both a psalm and a prophecy. Zechariah sings of hopes and promises in a world that waits in darkness and the shadow of death.

The scene surrounding John's birth is filled with echoes of the Old Testament. The ancient traditions of circumcising and naming the child are followed. Yet, like springtime in winter, God is doing something new. The hillsides resound with new songs of God's salvation. Zechariah thought he was too old for dreaming, too old for raising a child, maybe even too old to sing. The mistrusting, disbelieving old man now sang with full and confident voice and gained new strength to raise his son to be "the prophet of the Most High."

A sense of anticipation rippled through the Judean countryside as people asked with amazement and fear, "What, then, will this child become?" (verse 66). The question anticipates the public mission of John the Baptist in the desert (verse 80). The Judean desert is only a short distance away, a barren steppe east of Jerusalem descending to the Jordan River. The time in the desert was the formative period for ancient Israel; the mission of John in the desert marks the end of the old covenant and the beginning of the new kingdom of God (Luke 16:16).

Reflection and discussion

• What do I think I am too old for? How might God prove me wrong?

• When Zechariah doubted, he became mute. How does trust open both my heart and my mouth?

• Am I skeptical or mistrusting of God's promises to me? Do I trust in the unknown future God has planned for me?

• His parents insisted that their son be named John (verses 59–63). Why was I given my name? What is the meaning of my name?

• Which verse or phrase of Zechariah's canticle most echoes in my heart? Why?

Prayer

Lord, God of Israel, you have done great things of old and you promise even greater things to come. Help me live my life in trusting confidence, anticipating the fulfillment of your promises.

Mary gave birth to her firstborn son and wrapped him in bands of cloth, and laid him in a manger, because there was no place for them in the inn. Luke 2:7

Bethlehem: Church of the Nativity

LUKE 2:1–7 *¹In those days a decree went out from Emperor Augustus that all the world should be registered. ²This was the first registration and was taken while Quirinius was governor of Syria. ³All went to their own towns to be registered. ⁴Joseph also went from the town of Nazareth in Galilee to Judea, to the city of David called Bethlehem, because he was descended from the house and family of David. ⁵He went to be registered with Mary, to whom he was engaged and who was expecting a child. ⁶While they were there, the time came for her to deliver her child. ⁷And she gave birth to her firstborn son and wrapped him in bands of cloth, and laid him in a manger, because there was no place for them in the inn.*

MATTHEW 2:1–11 *¹In the time of King Herod, after Jesus was born in Bethlehem of Judea, wise men from the East came to Jerusalem, ²asking, "Where is the child who has been born king of the Jews? For we observed his star at its rising, and have come to pay him homage." ³When King Herod heard this, he was frightened, and all Jerusalem with him; ⁴and calling together all the chief priests and scribes of the people, he inquired of them where the Messiah was to be born. ⁵They told him, "In Bethlehem of Judea; for so it has been written by the prophet:*

⁶'And you, Bethlehem, in the land of Judah,
      are by no means least among the rulers of Judah;
      for from you shall come a ruler
         who is to shepherd my people Israel.'"
⁷Then Herod secretly called for the wise men and learned from them the exact time when the star had appeared. ⁸Then he sent them to Bethlehem, saying, "Go and search diligently for the child; and when you have found him, bring me word so that I may also go and pay him homage."
⁹When they had heard the king, they set out; and there, ahead of them, went the star that they had seen at its rising, until it stopped over the place where the child was. ¹⁰When they saw that the star had stopped, they were overwhelmed with joy. ¹¹On entering the house, they saw the child with Mary his mother; and they knelt down and paid him homage. Then, opening their treasure chests, they offered him gifts of gold, frankincense, and myrrh.

Both the gospels of Luke and Matthew tell us that Jesus was born in Bethlehem. Luke explains that a census of the empire had been ordered, thus everyone was to return to the place of his family roots. Joseph returned to Bethlehem since he was a descendent of King David whose hometown was Bethlehem (Luke 2:4). It was expected that the Messiah would come from "the line of David," and that the birthplace of Israel's greatest king was to be the birthplace of the King of kings (1 Sam 16; Mic 5:1; Matt 2:4–6).

After the earthly life of Jesus, his relatives in Bethlehem and the first century Judeo-Christians preserved the memory of his place of birth. Justin Martyr, writing in the middle of the second century, stated that Jesus was born in a cave and that its location is generally accepted by those living in the area. In the fourth century, the emperor Constantine ordered the construction of a magnificent basilica over the cave of Christ's birth. Its four rows of columns formed five aisles, at the eastern end of which was an octagonal structure above the site of the grotto. Destroyed in the sixth century, the church was rebuilt by the emperor Justinian. The structure of that church still stands, but only a few fragments of its magnificent mosaics and golden embellishments remain.

A stairway in the sanctuary descends to the Cave of the Nativity where a silver star, glistening with the reflection of scores of oil lamps, marks the spot honored as the birthplace of Jesus. The star is inscribed with the Latin words

Hic De Virgine Maria Jesus Christus Natus Est (Here, of the Virgin Mary, Jesus Christ was born). A few feet away is the altar honoring the Adoration of the Magi and the site of the manger where the infant Jesus lay.

Surely the Son of God could have chosen whatever culture and economic strata he wanted to enter our world. We stand in wonder at the choice he made for himself, a choice which must have been for our benefit and our instruction. Since there was no place in the lodging for travelers, Mary and Joseph withdrew to a place where animals were kept, perhaps underneath or at the back of a house (Luke 2:7). The earliest tradition says the place of Jesus' birth was a cave, a natural place for keeping animals and their feed.

Bethlehem reminds us that God chooses the least likely places and people to bring us salvation: the smallest village, the lowliest manger, the simplest shepherds, a tiny child born in an obscure corner of the ancient world. The spacious entry of the Church of the Nativity was reduced to a small four-foot tall opening centuries ago to prevent looting on horseback. It seems appropriate that pilgrims should have to bow low to enter the place where God humbled himself to come among us.

Reflection and discussion

• According to the ancient Scriptures, why was Jesus destined to be born in Bethlehem?

• What emotions would Mary and Joseph have felt as the time came to have their child?

• What does the place of Jesus' birth teach me about human life and God's ways?

• What gift would I have brought to the newborn king? What is the best gift I have ever received?

• What might have been the favorite memory of Joseph and Mary at Bethlehem? What is my favorite memory of Christmas?

Prayer

Incarnate Son of God, you became like us in our humanity so that we could become like you in your divinity. Let me experience the tender love that you found in the arms of Mary.

In that region there were shepherds living in the fields, keeping watch over their flock by night. Luke 2:8

Bethlehem: Shepherd's Field

LUKE 2:8–20 ⁸*In that region there were shepherds living in the fields, keeping watch over their flock by night. ⁹Then an angel of the Lord stood before them, and the glory of the Lord shone around them, and they were terrified. ¹⁰But the angel said to them, "Do not be afraid; for see—I am bringing you good news of great joy for all the people: ¹¹to you is born this day in the city of David a Savior, who is the Messiah, the Lord. ¹²This will be a sign for you: you will find a child wrapped in bands of cloth and lying in a manger." ¹³And suddenly there was with the angel a multitude of the heavenly host, praising God and saying,*

    ¹⁴*"Glory to God in the highest heaven,*
      and on earth peace among those whom he favors!"

  ¹⁵*When the angels had left them and gone into heaven, the shepherds said to one another, "Let us go now to Bethlehem and see this thing that has taken place, which the Lord has made known to us." ¹⁶So they went with haste and found Mary and Joseph, and the child lying in the manger. ¹⁷When they saw this, they made known what had been told them about this child; ¹⁸and all who heard it were amazed at what the shepherds told them. ¹⁹But Mary treasured all these words and pondered them in her heart. ²⁰The shepherds returned, glorifying and praising God for all they had heard and seen, as it had been told them.*

To the east of the town of Bethlehem are the fields in which the shepherds watched their sheep on that holy night when Christ was born. Throughout the fields there are traces of chapels and monasteries dating back to the fifth century which served pilgrims on their way to Bethlehem. Nestled in a natural glen is the Grotto of the Shepherds, a natural cave that has been converted into a small chapel, its walls and altar of natural, uncut stone. On the knoll above the cave is the small, round Shepherd's Field Church, in the shape of a nomad's tent. The dome is studded with round glass blocks which break up the sunlight into dancing rainbow colors.

The shepherds remind us of David, the shepherd king. When David was tending his flock near the town of Bethlehem, he was chosen as king and anointed (1 Sam 16:11). God said to David, "It is you who shall be shepherd of my people Israel" (2 Sam 5:2).

At the time of Jesus, shepherds were people of low esteem. They were poor nomads, often looked upon with suspicion, holding no social or religious status in Israel. That they would be chosen as the first to hear the "good news of great joy" (verse 10) is surely an indication that God has "lifted up the lowly" (1:52). Jesus' birth among the poor anticipates his ministry to the poor and outcasts of Israel's society. He whose birth was first announced to shepherd in the fields, will become the good shepherd of the sheep.

The angel's announcement is the message of the entire gospel: the one born in Bethlehem is Savior, Messiah, and Lord (verse 11). Yet the "sign"—a baby swaddled in bands of cloth and lying in a manger—is not what one would expect at the birth of such a child. Both the announcement of his sovereignty and the simplicity of the sign invite us to ponder the mystery of this humble Savior.

Around the circumference of the church's dome is written in large, golden letters: *Gloria In Altissimis Deo, Et In Terra Pax Hominibus Bonae Voluntatis* (Glory to God in the Highest, and on Earth Peace to People of Good Will). The canticle of the angels, the Gloria (verse 14), proclaims that heaven has touched earth in this wondrous birth. God in heaven is given glory; people on earth are brought peace.

Reflection and discussion

• Why did God proclaim to the shepherds what kings and priests longed to hear?

• Is my life simple and humble enough to hear God's good news?

• How was the life of the shepherds changed that night as they moved from fear to fascination?

Prayer

Prince of Peace, you were born in an obscure village and visited by humble shepherds. I come to you as I am, unembarrassed, because you have chosen neither wealth nor royalty nor power, but a simple manger. Give me the peace which the angels announced and let me give you glory.

SUGGESTIONS FOR FACILITATORS, GROUP SESSION 2

1. If there are newcomers who were not present for the first group session, introduce them now.

2. You may want to pray this prayer as a group:
O Word by which the whole creation came to be, you were conceived of the Holy Spirit in the womb of Mary in the town of Nazareth. Her journey into the hill country caused Elizabeth to cry out in amazement and her unborn son to leap with joy. The announcement of your angel brought songs of joy to the land. Mary and Zechariah sang their canticles. The angels of God sang in thunderous chorus in the fields of Bethlehem. Angels descending to the earth and human voices ascending to the skies—what a wondrous harmony your coming brings into the world! Fill us with your peace as we, like Mary, treasure all these words and ponder them in our hearts.

3. Ask one or more of the following questions:
• What was your biggest challenge in Bible study over this past week?
• What is the most important lesson you learned in your study this week?

4. Discuss lessons 1 through 6 together. Assuming that group members have read the Scripture and commentary during the week, there is no need to read it aloud. As you review each lesson, you might want to briefly summarize the Scripture passages of each lesson and ask the group what stands out most clearly about each pilgrimage location.

5. Choose one or more of the questions for reflection and discussion from each lesson to talk over as a group. You may want to ask group members which question was most challenging or helpful to them as you review each lesson.

6. Keep the discussion moving, but don't rush it in order to complete more questions. Allow time for the questions that provoke the most discussion.

7. Instruct group members to complete lessons 7 through 12 on their own during the six days before the next group meeting. They should write out their own answers to the questions as preparation for next week's session.

8. Conclude by praying aloud together the prayer at the end of lesson 6, or any other prayer you choose.

John went into all the regions around the Jordan, proclaiming a baptism of repentance for the forgiveness of sins. Luke 3:3

The Jordan River: Place of Baptism

LUKE 3:1–22 *¹In the fifteenth year of the reign of Emperor Tiberius, when Pontius Pilate was governor of Judea, and Herod was ruler of Galilee, and his brother Philip ruler of the region of Ituraea and Trachonitis, and Lysanias ruler of Abilene, ²during the high priesthood of Annas and Caiaphas, the word of God came to John son of Zechariah in the wilderness. ³He went into all the region around the Jordan, proclaiming a baptism of repentance for the forgiveness of sins, ⁴as it is written in the book of the words of the prophet Isaiah,*

"The voice of one crying out in the wilderness:
'Prepare the way of the Lord,
make his paths straight.
⁵Every valley shall be filled,
and every mountain and hill shall be made low,
and the crooked shall be made straight,
and the rough ways made smooth;
⁶and all flesh shall see the salvation of God.'"

⁷John said to the crowds that came out to be baptized by him, "You brood of vipers! Who warned you to flee from the wrath to come? ⁸Bear fruits worthy of

30

repentance. *Do not begin to say to yourselves, 'We have Abraham as our ancestor'; for I tell you, God is able from these stones to raise up children to Abraham.* ⁹*Even now the ax is lying at the root of the trees; every tree therefore that does not bear good fruit is cut down and thrown into the fire."*

¹⁰*And the crowds asked him, "What then should we do?"* ¹¹*In reply he said to them, "Whoever has two coats must share with anyone who has none; and whoever has food must do likewise."* ¹²*Even tax collectors came to be baptized, and they asked him, "Teacher, what should we do?"* ¹³*He said to them, "Collect no more than the amount prescribed for you."* ¹⁴*Soldiers also asked him, "And we, what should we do?" He said to them, "Do not extort money from anyone by threats or false accusation, and be satisfied with your wages."*

¹⁵*As the people were filled with expectation, and all were questioning in their hearts concerning John, whether he might be the Messiah,* ¹⁶*John answered all of them by saying, "I baptize you with water; but one who is more powerful than I is coming; I am not worthy to untie the thong of his sandals. He will baptize you with the Holy Spirit and fire.* ¹⁷*His winnowing fork is in his hand, to clear his threshing floor and to gather the wheat into his granary; but the chaff he will burn with unquenchable fire."*

¹⁸*So, with many other exhortations, he proclaimed the good news to the people.* ¹⁹*But Herod the ruler, who had been rebuked by him because of Herodias, his brother's wife, and because of all the evil things that Herod had done,* ²⁰*added to them all by shutting up John in prison.*

²¹*Now when all the people were baptized, and when Jesus also had been baptized and was praying, the heaven was opened,* ²²*and the Holy Spirit descended upon him in bodily form like a dove. And a voice came from heaven, "You are my Son, the Beloved; with you I am well pleased."*

The flowing water of the Jordan River is the lifeblood of the Promised Land. The word "Jordan" is rooted in a word that means "to descend." The river begins in the north with its sources near the 9,000 foot high Mount Hermon and descends rapidly, flowing into the Sea of Galilee. Exiting the Sea of Galilee, the river continues to descend, finally flowing into the Dead Sea, the lowest point on the earth. For centuries pilgrims have gone to the Jordan River to be baptized or to renew their baptism.

As the Israelites concluded their journey through the desert after the exodus, they entered the Promised Land through the Jordan River (Joshua 3—

4). Passing through the Jordan was the defining moment that assured their freedom and gave them a new identity as the people of the land God had promised. Over 1200 years later, a Jewish prophet called John the Baptist summoned people to this same wilderness along the Jordan River to reenact Israel's defining moment. As John plunged people into the river, he was renewing their identity as God's people and bringing them into a new covenant as God's kingdom drew near.

John the Baptist was that voice crying out in the desert, preparing the way of the Lord, as Isaiah had prophesied (verse 4). It is possible that John once belonged to the community at Qumran. The ruins of that community have been excavated near the Dead Sea and the writings of that community are commonly known as the Dead Sea Scrolls. This apocalyptic Jewish community used this same passage from Isaiah (40:3–5) to explain why their community went to the desert.

John called people to repentance; yet the practical consequences of that change of heart is different for each person. For some it means giving clothing and food to those who have none (verse 11); for the tax collector it means to stop collecting more than is prescribed (verse 13); for a soldier it means being just (verse 14). Like those of John's time, we must ask, "What then should we do?" (verse 10) in order to express repentance for the forgiveness of sins.

The baptism of John expressed hope for forgiveness from God; the baptism promised in Jesus includes forgiveness of sin but also an indwelling of the Holy Spirit that leads to eternal life (verse 16). Christian baptism is the defining moment at the beginning of our Christian pilgrimage. In the waters we are set free and given a new identity as people of the Promised Land.

Reflection and discussion

• What are the practical consequences of a change of heart for me? What then should I do (verse 10) to express repentance?

• What ancient significance did the Jordan River have for John the Baptist? Why did he choose to baptize there?

• What does water symbolize for me? Why is water the essential element of Christian baptism?

•

• What new appreciation of baptism might I have if I understand it as the formal beginning of my Christian pilgrimage?

Prayer

Father of life, you proclaimed Jesus as your Son at his baptism in the Jordan. I want to live as your child, to call you Abba, to confess Jesus as Lord, and to live the good news of the kingdom.

"Everyone serves the good wine first, but
you have kept the good wine until now." John 2:10

Cana: Church of the Miracle of Water and Wine

JOHN 2:1–12 ¹*On the third day there was a wedding in Cana of Galilee, and the mother of Jesus was there.* ²*Jesus and his disciples had also been invited to the wedding.* ³*When the wine gave out, the mother of Jesus said to him, "They have no wine."* ⁴*And Jesus said to her, "Woman, what concern is that to you and to me? My hour has not yet come."* ⁵*His mother said to the servants, "Do whatever he tells you."* ⁶*Now standing there were six stone water jars for the Jewish rites of purification, each holding twenty or thirty gallons.* ⁷*Jesus said to them, "Fill the jars with water." And they filled them up to the brim.* ⁸*He said to them, "Now draw some out, and take it to the chief steward." So they took it.* ⁹*When the steward tasted the water that had become wine, and did not know where it came from (though the servants who had drawn the water knew), the steward called the bridegroom* ¹⁰*and said to him, "Everyone serves the good wine first, and then the inferior wine after the guests have become drunk. But you have kept the good wine until now."* ¹¹*Jesus did this, the first of his signs, in Cana of Galilee, and revealed his glory; and his disciples believed in him.*

¹²*After this he went down to Capernaum with his mother, his brothers, and his disciples; and they remained there a few days.*

The small town of Cana is a short distance from Nazareth. The Franciscan church, sometimes called the Wedding Church, commemorates the wedding that Jesus, Mary, and his disciples attended toward the beginning of Jesus' ministry. Weddings are often performed here and married pilgrims often renew their wedding vows at this place where Jesus honored marriage with his presence.

The wedding feast shows us that Jesus was not a desert ascetic like John the Baptist. He celebrated with people, and abundant life and joy seemed to characterize much of his life. On one level, the story of Cana is easy to understand. Jesus helped a couple who would have been embarrassed when the wine ran out at their wedding party. Yet the events told in John's gospel always have multiple layers of significance. Mary's request that Jesus provide wine for the feast (verse 3) was, on a deeper level, a request that Jesus bring about the abundant life and joy of the messianic banquet expected in the age to come.

The miracle signals the kind of radical change that Jesus represents. Never again would life be as predictable, bland, and colorless as water; life in Jesus becomes vibrant, luscious, and effervescent. Jesus has come to show people what they have been missing. The steward of the wedding feast joked to the bridegroom that he had waited to serve the best wine last (verse 10). Estimates of the size of the stone water jars at Cana indicate that the amount of choice wine produced was well over a hundred gallons (verses 6–7).

"Too much of a good thing is wonderful," Mae West once quipped. The first miracle of Jesus shocked the wedding guests with an extravagance of the finest quality wine. The prophets had described God's future blessings as an abundance of wine. The day is surely coming, said the prophet, when, "the mountains shall drip sweet wine and all the hills shall flow with it" (Amos 9:13). The profusion of God's future blessings is without limits. "I came that they may have life, and have it abundantly," Jesus said (John 10:10).

The changing of the water into wine was the first of the seven "signs" of Jesus in John's gospel. A sign is not merely a miraculous wonder, but a revelation of who Jesus is and an invitation to faith in him (verse 11). Though Jesus responded to Mary, "My hour has not yet come" (verse 4), Jesus anticipated the hour of his death and resurrection with this display of blessings, joy, and love for others. Marriage and the whole of Christian life anticipates the eternal banquet of God's kingdom.

Reflection and discussion

• Am I trusting enough to do whatever Jesus tells me to do (verse 5)?

• In what ways does the wine at Cana express the life which Jesus offers me?

• How could a renewed relationship with Jesus show me the abundant life I may be missing?

Prayer

Lord of the age to come, you turn water into wine and transform ordinary existence into abundant living. Manifest your power in my life today and let me see the signs of God's presence all around me.

They came to Capernaum; and when the Sabbath came, Jesus entered the synagogue and taught. Mark 1:21

Capernaum: The Synagogue

MARK 1:21–28 *²¹ They went to Capernaum; and when the sabbath came, he entered the synagogue and taught. ²² They were astounded at his teaching, for he taught them as one having authority, and not as the scribes. ²³ Just then there was in their synagogue a man with an unclean spirit, ²⁴ and he cried out, "What have you to do with us, Jesus of Nazareth? Have you come to destroy us? I know who you are, the Holy One of God." ²⁵ But Jesus rebuked him, saying, "Be silent, and come out of him!" ²⁶ And the unclean spirit, convulsing him and crying with a loud voice, came out of him. ²⁷ They were all amazed, and they kept on asking one another, "What is this? A new teaching—with authority! He commands even the unclean spirits, and they obey him." ²⁸ At once his fame began to spread throughout the surrounding region of Galilee.*

JOHN 6:53–59 *⁵³ So Jesus said to them, "Very truly, I tell you, unless you eat the flesh of the Son of Man and drink his blood, you have no life in you. ⁵⁴ Those who eat my flesh and drink my blood have eternal life, and I will raise them up on the last day; ⁵⁵ for my flesh is true food and my blood is true drink. ⁵⁶ Those who eat my flesh and drink my blood abide in me, and I in them. ⁵⁷ Just as the living Father sent* *me, and I live because of the Father, so whoever eats me will live because of me.* [58] *This is the bread that came down from heaven, not like that which your ancestors ate, and they died. But the one who eats this bread will live forever." * [59] *He said these things while he was teaching in the synagogue at Capernaum.*

In the days of Jesus, Capernaum was an important town along the northern shores of the Sea of Galilee. It was a center for the fishing industry and a post for tax collection. Nearby Jesus called at least five of his disciples to follow him: Peter, Andrew, James, John, and Matthew (or Levi). Matthew's gospel refers to Capernaum as Jesus' "own town" (Matt 9:1); it was the hub of his ministry in the region of Galilee.

Capernaum has been excavated, revealing some fascinating ruins. The most obvious is the fifth-century synagogue, which was built over the first-century synagogue where Jesus taught and healed. Jewish images are seen on the carved ruins; among them are the *shofar* (ram's horn), an incense shovel, a *menorah* (seven-branched candelabrum), and a representation of the Ark of the Covenant. There were two centers for Jewish spiritual life in the time of Jesus: the Temple, seventy-five miles away in Jerusalem, was the place of sacrifice and pilgrim feasts; the synagogue, found in every town, was the place for Scripture reading, teaching, and prayer.

The first-century synagogue which Jesus and his disciples frequented was made of black basalt stones. These can be seen beneath the white limestone of the present ruins. This synagogue was built by a Roman centurion (Luke 7:5). When this centurion's servant was on the verge of death, he sent for Jesus to come. A man of great humility and trust, he said to Jesus, "Lord, I am not worthy to have you come under my roof, but only speak the word and let my servant be healed" (Luke 7:6–7). Jesus was amazed at such faith, praised him to his followers, and healed his servant.

Jesus taught in this synagogue with an authority which his listeners knew was from God (Mark 1:21–22, 27). Here he healed the man with the unclean spirit, which caused his fame to spread throughout Galilee (Mark 1:23–28). The gospel of John tells us that Jesus delivered his Bread of Life discourse while teaching in the Capernaum synagogue (John 6:59). The words that Jesus spoke here were not written on the Torah scrolls of the synagogue; they were a new word of God. Capernaum with its synagogue has fallen into ruin, but this word endures forever.

Reflection and discussion

• Why did Jesus call his disciples from among the fishermen and tax collectors of Capernaum?

• What might have been the reaction of those who heard the Bread of Life discourse of Jesus in the synagogue (John 6:59)?

• What is the difference between the temple and a synagogue at the time of Jesus?

Prayer

Jesus, you taught in the synagogue with a new authority. Give me the faith of the centurion, help me to listen carefully to your words, and give me the confidence to follow you faithfully because you alone have the words of everlasting life.

As soon as they left the synagogue, they entered the house of Simon and Andrew, with James and John. Mark 1:29

Capernaum: Peter's House

MARK 1:29–34 ²⁹*As soon as they left the synagogue, they entered the house of Simon and Andrew, with James and John.* ³⁰*Now Simon's mother-in-law was in bed with a fever, and they told him about her at once.* ³¹*He came and took her by the hand and lifted her up. Then the fever left her, and she began to serve them.*

³²*That evening, at sundown, they brought to him all who were sick or possessed with demons.* ³³*And the whole city was gathered around the door.* ³⁴*And he cured many who were sick with various diseases, and cast out many demons; and he would not permit the demons to speak, because they knew him.*

MARK 2:1–12 ¹*When he returned to Capernaum after some days, it was reported that he was at home.* ²*So many gathered around that there was no longer room for them, not even in front of the door; and he was speaking the word to them.* ³*Then some people came, bringing to him a paralyzed man, carried by four of them.* ⁴*And when they could not bring him to Jesus because of the crowd, they removed the roof above him; and after having dug through it, they let down the mat on which the paralytic lay.* ⁵*When Jesus saw their faith, he said to the paralytic, "Son, your sins are forgiven."* ⁶*Now some of the scribes were sitting there, questioning in their hearts,* ⁷*"Why does this fellow speak in this way? It is blasphemy! Who can forgive sins but God alone?"* ⁸*At once Jesus perceived* *in his spirit that they were discussing these questions among themselves; and he said to them, "Why do you raise such questions in your hearts? ⁹Which is easier, to say to the paralytic, 'Your sins are forgiven,' or to say, 'Stand up and take your mat and walk'? ¹⁰But so that you may know that the Son of Man has authority on earth to forgive sins" —he said to the paralytic— ¹¹"I say to you, stand up, take your mat and go to your home." ¹²And he stood up, and immediately took the mat and went out before all of them; so that they were all amazed and glorified God, saying, "We have never seen anything like this!"*

A short distance from the synagogue are the remains of Peter's house. Similar to the other houses in Capernaum at the time of Jesus, it had one large room, measuring about twenty feet by twenty feet, and several smaller rooms. The walls of the house were built of black basalt stones, and the roof was made of clay and straw.

This house of Peter and his family was the place Jesus called "home" after leaving Nazareth (Mark 2:1; 3:19–20). Here Jesus returned at the end of each day, relaxed with his disciples, planned for the next day, talking with his friends into the night. Here, too, people came seeking Jesus—the sick, the possessed, and all who were in need (1:32–34). They knew they could find in Jesus a refreshing word, a healing touch, a saving presence. Here the four friends of the paralyzed man dug out panels from the roof and lowered him on a mat to the feet of Jesus because of the crowds (2:3–4). Jesus must have smiled at this beautiful expression of trusting friendship.

Bringing another to Jesus is the deepest expression of friendship. Sometimes people are unable to come to Jesus on their own, if not because of paralysis as in the gospel account, because of fear, insecurity, or shame.

After the life of Jesus, the house of Peter became a gathering place for celebrating Eucharist among the early Christians. In the second half of the first century, the walls and ceilings of the large room of the house were plastered to create a church. On this plaster are etched writings from early pilgrims such as "Christ have mercy" and "Lord Jesus, help your servant." In the fifth century an eight-sided church was built around and over Peter's house. This octagonal style was popular in the Byzantine period, and allowed worshippers to form a procession around the holy site.

Today a modern church is built upon pillars over the ruins. In the center of the church, a glass floor allows visitors to look into the excavations below and stand directly above the place which Jesus called home. As pilgrims worship in this church, they are able to feel the life of Jesus as close as anywhere on earth.

Reflection and discussion

• Are there any similarities between the place Jesus called home and my own home?

• What is sacred about the place I call home?

• The four friends brought the paralyzed man to Jesus. In what ways am I able to bring another person to Jesus?

Prayer

Lord Jesus, the house of Peter became your home on earth, a place in which others received forgiveness and healing. Help me to make my home a comfortable place where others can find rest, hospitality, and help in time of need.

Taking the five loaves and the two fish, Jesus looked up to heaven,
and blessed and broke the loaves, and gave them
to the disciple to set before the people. Mark 6:41

Tabgha: Church of the Multiplication of Loaves and Fishes

MARK 6:30–44 *⁣³⁰The apostles gathered around Jesus, and told him all that they had done and taught. ³¹He said to them, "Come away to a deserted place all by yourselves and rest a while." For many were coming and going, and they had no leisure even to eat. ³²And they went away in the boat to a deserted place by themselves. ³³Now many saw them going and recognized them, and they hurried there on foot from all the towns and arrived ahead of them. ³⁴As he went ashore, he saw a great crowd; and he had compassion for them, because they were like sheep without a shepherd; and he began to teach them many things. ³⁵When it grew late, his disciples came to him and said, "This is a deserted place, and the hour is now very late; ³⁶send them away so that they may go into the surrounding country and villages and buy something for themselves to eat." ³⁷But he answered them, "You give them something to eat." They said to him, "Are we to go and buy two hundred denarii worth of bread, and give it to them to eat?" ³⁸And he said to them, "How many loaves have you? Go and see." When they had found out, they said, "Five, and two fish." ³⁹Then he ordered them to get all the people to sit down in groups on the green grass. ⁴⁰So they sat down in groups of* *hundreds and of fifties.* ⁴¹ *Taking the five loaves and the two fish, he looked up to heaven, and blessed and broke the loaves, and gave them to his disciples to set before the people; and he divided the two fish among them all.* ⁴² *And all ate and were filled;* ⁴³ *and they took up twelve baskets full of broken pieces and of the fish.* ⁴⁴ *Those who had eaten the loaves numbered five thousand men.*

The fields where Jesus multiplied the loaves and the fish for the hungry crowds are traditionally located on the northwest shore of the Sea of Galilee. The place is called Tabgha, derived from "Place of Seven Springs," named for the fresh waters that flow through the area into the Sea of Galilee. A chapel was built there in the fourth century to commemorate the miracle, and in the fifth century a Byzantine church was built on the site. Destroyed in the seventh century, the remains were covered until they were rediscovered in the early part of the twentieth century.

A new church was built in 1982 following the ancient Byzantine architectural style. Visitors first enter a peaceful atrium which serves as a transition zone from the outside world before entering the sanctuary for prayer. The austere interior is marked by soaring arches and massive stone columns. The early mosaic artistry on the floor has been preserved and restored, including the famous loaves and fish mosaic in front of the altar.

The miracle of the multiplication is the only miracle recorded in all four gospels. Mark tells us that Jesus was moved to pity at the crowd that was "like sheep without a shepherd." His initial response is not to feed them with food but to teach them many things (verse 34). Israel's wisdom tradition associated feeding and eating bread with teaching and learning (Prov 9:5; Sir 15:3).

Mark's readers realize that the teaching of Jesus is as important for life as bread in the wilderness was for their ancestors in the exodus. Though the disciples could not understand how the hungry crowds could be fed, the meager loaves and fishes fed the crowd of five thousand. The twelve baskets were one for each of the twelve disciples. They would each have the task of feeding those who are like sheep without a shepherd when Jesus has risen.

The actions of Jesus are described in language that foreshadows his final meal on the eve of his own death. The feeding accounts in each gospel and the Last Supper narratives describe Jesus as taking, blessing, breaking, and giving the bread. An early tradition maintains that Jesus placed the five loaves and two fish on a rock before feeding the hungry crowds. This rock is preserved today beneath the altar of the present church, emphasizing the continuity of the miraculous feeding with every eucharistic celebration through the ages. In every eucharist Jesus feeds the deepest hungers of his pilgrim people with the living word and with the bread of life.

Reflection and discussion

• What does the miracle of the loaves and fishes teach me about my own hungers?

• What do the twelve baskets teach about the church's responsibility to feed the physical and spiritual hungers of people today?

• In what way are the words of Jesus, "You give them something to eat" (verse 37), directed to me?

Prayer

Lord of life, you satisfy the hungry heart. May I not neglect my spiritual health with food that does not nourish me. Thank you for the sustenance of your word and the nourishment of your life.

When Jesus saw the crowds, he went up the mountain; and after he sat down, his disciples came to him. Matt 5:1

Mount of Beatitudes: Church of the Beatitudes

MATTHEW 5:1–16 ¹*When Jesus saw the crowds, he went up the mountain; and after he sat down, his disciples came to him.* ²*Then he began to speak, and taught them, saying:*

³*"Blessed are the poor in spirit, for theirs is the kingdom of heaven.*

⁴*Blessed are those who mourn, for they will be comforted.*

⁵*Blessed are the meek, for they will inherit the earth.*

⁶*Blessed are those who hunger and thirst for righteousness,*
for they will be filled.

⁷*Blessed are the merciful, for they will receive mercy.*

⁸*Blessed are the pure in heart, for they will see God.*

⁹*Blessed are the peacemakers, for they will be called children of God.*

¹⁰*Blessed are those who are persecuted for righteousness' sake,*
for theirs is the kingdom of heaven.

¹¹*Blessed are you when people revile you and persecute you*
and utter all kinds of evil against you falsely on my account.

¹²*Rejoice and be glad, for your reward is great in heaven,*

for in the same way they persecuted the prophets who were before you.

[13] *"You are the salt of the earth; but if salt has lost its taste, how can its saltiness be restored? It is no longer good for anything, but is thrown out and trampled under foot.*

[14] *"You are the light of the world. A city built on a hill cannot be hid.* [15] *No one after lighting a lamp puts it under the bushel basket, but on the lampstand, and it gives light to all in the house.* [16] *In the same way, let your light shine before others, so that they may see your good works and give glory to your Father in heaven."*

O n a hilltop above the northwestern part of the Sea of Galilee is a beautiful chapel dedicated to Jesus' Sermon on the Mount. Its eight-sided cupola commemorates the eight beatitudes which introduce the sermon. The gardens outside the church are ideal for tranquil reflection, and the panorama offers an encompassing view of the Sea of Galilee and the region of Jesus' ministry.

The Sermon on the Mount (Matt 5–7) has been called a "blueprint for Christian holiness." On the mountain Jesus is the new Moses, teaching a law of holiness that magnifies but does not replace the ancient law of Israel. The gentle beauty of this mountain contrasts with the fiery and thunderous Mount Sinai. Moses had warned the people not to come near the mountain, but Jesus invites his disciples up the mount to listen.

Jesus used forms of speech that were simple and easy to memorize. One of these teaching devices is a beatitude. There are over 250 beatitudes in the Bible, mostly in the Old Testament. A beatitude is a saying which begins with the word "blessed," then usually identifies the kind of person who is blessed, and often concludes with the reason why this kind of person can be considered blessed. The eight beatitudes of Jesus have been handed to us because they are simple, clear, and memorable. They proclaim the inner attitudes or ways of living that characterize a follower of Jesus: humble, single-minded, seeking justice, and willing to undergo persecution for the sake of Jesus.

The view of the lush Galilee region from this mount shows us the world that surrounded Jesus. He observed the sower, the harvester, and the vine-grower. He learned the secrets of the fig tree, the briar, the sycamore, and the tiny mustard seed. He saw the ways of the birds building their nests, the foxes hiding in their shelters, and flowers of the field arrayed in vibrant color. All these images came to life in the teachings and parables of Jesus.

The beautiful shrine on the mount and its tranquil setting reminds us that the way of Jesus outlined in his sermon gives us contentment and peace. Jesus taught a message that is not easy; yet one which makes us truly blessed and deeply happy.

Reflection and discussion

• Do I consider myself as truly blessed? Which one of the beatitudes most characterizes my life?

• Which of the beatitudes do I most want to focus on living today?

• What does the natural world teach me about God and God's will for me?

Prayer

Teacher and Lord, you show me the way to a blessed and happy life. Open my ears to your teaching so that I may learn and follow your way. Thank you for inviting me to be your disciple.

SUGGESTIONS FOR FACILITATORS, GROUP SESSION 3

1. Welcome group members and ask if there are any announcements anyone would like to make.

2. You may want to pray this prayer as a group:
Lord Jesus, as we follow in your footsteps, you have brought us from the desert, to the seaside, and to the mountain. The created world is charged with divine goodness and love. You are the giver of all good gifts and the source of those things that we most deeply desire. As we gather as your people, encourage us to listen to God's word, allow it to penetrate our hearts, and give us the confidence necessary to put it into practice in our daily lives. Bless us with your Holy Spirit as we learn about you together.

3. Ask one or more of the following questions:
   • What did you learn about Jesus from your study this week?
   • What did you learn about yourself this week?

4. Discuss lessons 7 through 12. Choose one or more of the questions for reflection and discussion from each lesson to talk over as a group. You may want to ask group members which question was most challenging or helpful to them as you review each lesson.

5. Remember that there are no definitive answers for these discussion questions. The insights of group members will add to the understanding of all. None of these questions require an expert.

6. After reviewing each lesson, instruct group members to complete lessons 13 through 18 on their own during the six days before the next group meeting. They should write out their own answers to the questions as preparation for next week's group meeting.

7. Ask the group if anyone is having any particular problems with his or her Bible study during the week. You may want to share advice and encouragement within the group.

8. Conclude by praying aloud together the prayer at the end of one of the lessons discussed. You may add to the prayer based on the sharing that has occurred in the group.

A gale arose on the lake, so great that the boat was being swamped by the waves; but Jesus was asleep. Matt 8:24

The Sea of Galilee

LUKE 5:1–11 *¹Once while Jesus was standing beside the lake of Gennesaret, and the crowd was pressing in on him to hear the word of God, ²he saw two boats there at the shore of the lake; the fishermen had gone out of them and were washing their nets. ³He got into one of the boats, the one belonging to Simon, and asked him to put out a little way from the shore. Then he sat down and taught the crowds from the boat. ⁴When he had finished speaking, he said to Simon, "Put out into the deep water and let down your nets for a catch." ⁵Simon answered, "Master, we have worked all night long but have caught nothing. Yet if you say so, I will let down the nets." ⁶When they had done this, they caught so many fish that their nets were beginning to break. ⁷So they signaled their partners in the other boat to come and help them. And they came and filled both boats, so that they began to sink. ⁸But when Simon Peter saw it, he fell down at Jesus' knees, saying, "Go away from me, Lord, for I am a sinful man!" ⁹For he and all who were with him were amazed at the catch of fish that they had taken; ¹⁰and so also were James and John, sons of Zebedee, who were partners with Simon. Then Jesus said to Simon, "Do not be afraid; from now on you will be catching people." ¹¹When they had brought their boats to shore, they left everything and followed him.*

MATTHEW 8: 23–27 ²³*And when he got into the boat, his disciples followed him.* ²⁴*A windstorm arose on the sea, so great that the boat was being swamped by the waves; but he was asleep.* ²⁵*And they went and woke him up, saying, "Lord, save us! We are perishing!"* ²⁶*And he said to them, "Why are you afraid, you of little faith?" Then he got up and rebuked the winds and the sea; and there was a dead calm.* ²⁷*They were amazed, saying, "What sort of man is this, that even the winds and the sea obey him?"*

MARK 6:45–52 ⁴⁵*Immediately he made his disciples get into the boat and go on ahead to the other side, to Bethsaida, while he dismissed the crowd.* ⁴⁶*After saying farewell to them, he went up on the mountain to pray.*

⁴⁷*When evening came, the boat was out on the sea, and he was alone on the land.* ⁴⁸*When he saw that they were straining at the oars against an adverse wind, he came towards them early in the morning, walking on the sea. He intended to pass them by.* ⁴⁹*But when they saw him walking on the sea, they thought it was a ghost and cried out;* ⁵⁰*for they all saw him and were terrified. But immediately he spoke to them and said, "Take heart, it is I; do not be afraid."* ⁵¹*Then he got into the boat with them and the wind ceased. And they were utterly astounded,* ⁵²*for they did not understand about the loaves, but their hearts were hardened.*

The Sea of Galilee is the heart of the Galilee region. It is sometimes called the Sea of Tiberias in the New Testament, named after the emperor Tiberius who ruled the Roman world during the public life of Jesus. The lake is known in the Old Testament as Kinneret, from the Hebrew kinnor (meaning harp) for that is its shape. The Sea is twelve miles in length and seven miles wide. It is usually calm with cool breezes, but sometimes sudden and violent storms turn it into a raging sea with high waves.

Near the Sea of Galilee Jesus conducted the greater part of his public ministry. He would often cross the sea to get from one town to another along the shores, or he would teach from a boat to the crowds on the shore (Luke 5:3). Luke's gospel describes the call of Peter in the context of a miraculous catch of fish (Luke 5:4–10). Peter must have been skilled at catching fish by trade, but Jesus called him to the work of catching people, gathering people into the kingdom of God. Still today many residents of the area gain a livelihood from fishing the well-stocked Sea. The so-called St. Peter fish (*musht*) is the best known and the tastiest. It can be enjoyed at local restaurants.

Jesus demonstrates that he has power over the wind and the waves, a power that belongs only to God (Matt 8:27). The boat tossing on the violent sea has become an image for the church; it can also be an apt image for our individual lives. When we seem to be on the verge of going under, we cry out to Jesus for salvation (Matt 8:25). Even when Jesus seems to be asleep, we know that he is with us and we are safe in his care.

Jesus' walking on water in the early hours of morning (Mark 6:48–49) demonstrates his divine power. Throughout the Bible God's power is said to conquer the forces of chaos and destruction symbolized by the sea. The darkness of night, the power of the waves, the appearance of the ghostly specter on the water, and the cries and fear of the disciples presents a dramatic scene, and a strong contrast to the calming words and actions of Jesus (Mark 6:50–51).

The Sea of Galilee is still alive with many fishing vessels. Pilgrims may take one of the local boats—some of them replicas of the first century fishing boats—to cross the Sea of Galilee. Whether the sea is tranquil or restless, an expedition to the middle of the lake by boat can be an inspirational experience. The sea is especially beautiful at night when the boats set out with their lamps alight.

Reflection and discussion

• Why would Jesus have chosen fishermen by the sea and not religious officials from the temple to be his disciples?

• When have I felt abandoned, in danger of being swamped by the waves?

• In what ways is the boat on the sea an apt image for the church? For my own life?

• What qualities of fishermen do I need for the work of "catching people" for God's kingdom (Luke 5:10)?

• What thoughts and emotions fill my mind and heart as I imagine the scene of Jesus walking on the sea?

Prayer

Lord of the wind and the sea, I cry out to you in fear when I feel like I am perishing. Help me to trust in your saving power, assure me that you are near, and save me from the forces that seek to overwhelm me.

When Jesus came into the district of Caesarea Philippi, he asked his disciples, "Who do people say that the Son of Man is?" Matt 16:13

Banias: Caesarea Philippi

MATTHEW 16:13–23 [13]*Now when Jesus came into the district of Caesarea Philippi, he asked his disciples, "Who do people say that the Son of Man is?"* [14]*And they said, "Some say John the Baptist, but others Elijah, and still others Jeremiah or one of the prophets."* [15]*He said to them, "But who do you say that I am?"* [16]*Simon Peter answered, "You are the Messiah, the Son of the living God."* [17]*And Jesus answered him, "Blessed are you, Simon son of Jonah! For flesh and blood has not revealed this to you, but my Father in heaven.* [18]*And I tell you, you are Peter, and on this rock I will build my church, and the gates of Hades will not prevail against it.* [19]*I will give you the keys of the kingdom of heaven, and whatever you bind on earth will be bound in heaven, and whatever you loose on earth will be loosed in heaven."* [20]*Then he sternly ordered the disciples not to tell anyone that he was the Messiah.*

[21]*From that time on, Jesus began to show his disciples that he must go to Jerusalem and undergo great suffering at the hands of the elders and chief priests and scribes, and be killed, and on the third day be raised.* [22]*And Peter took him aside and began to rebuke him, saying, "God forbid it, Lord! This must never happen to you."* [23]*But he turned and said to Peter, "Get behind me, Satan! You*

are a stumbling block to me; for you are setting your mind not on divine things but on human things."

Caesarea Philippi was a city in the northernmost part of Galilee on the southern slope of Mount Hermon, the highest mountain in the Holy Land. One of the three springs which feeds the Jordan River is here and the Hermon River flows through the area and into the Jordan. The Greeks dedicated the cave from which the spring flows to the deity Pan and named the city Paneas. The Romans later assigned the district to Herod the Great who erected a temple to Augustus there, placing the image of the emperor near the altar of Pan. After Herod's death, his son Philip beautified the city and named it Caesarea. It became known as Caesarea Philippi (the Caesar city of Philip) to distinguish it from the city with the same name on the Mediterranean coast.

In New Testament times Caesarea Philippi was a place to worship Pan and to honor Caesar. Today the area is a beautiful nature reserve, alive with flowing water and vegetation. It was in this pastoral and cultic setting that Jesus asked the crucial question of his disciples: "Who do you say that I am?" (verse 15). The question remains through the ages as a living challenge to be answered by all disciples.

Jesus is called by many names and titles throughout the gospels. The Jews of the time had many ideas about the messianic figure for whom they hoped: an ideal king descended from David, a great prophet like Moses, a priestly messiah, and others. As the New Testament writings reveal, Jesus fulfilled all of these expectations, yet not in the way people hoped.

Looking at the escarpment above the cave of Pan, we can understand why the metaphor of "the rock" suggested itself to Jesus. After Simon Peter answered, "You are the Messiah, the Son of the living God" (verse 16), Jesus proclaimed him "the rock" on which the church would be built (verse 18). The rocky foundation for the church of Jesus would not be the rock of Jerusalem, the rock upon which the great temple was built. The rock would be Peter and the faith in Jesus which he professed. The keys to the kingdom and the power to bind and loose refer to a unique teaching authority and decision-making authority given to Peter for the sake of the church (verse 19).

But the faith of Peter is not yet complete. Here in this northern city most distant from Jerusalem, Jesus reveals for the first time that he had to go to Jerusalem and there to suffer and give up his life (verses 21–22). At this turning point in the gospel, Peter's rebuke of Jesus indicates that he still has much to learn as he begins to make his way toward Jerusalem with Jesus.

Reflection and discussion

• Why did Jesus choose Caesarea-Philippi to reveal his identity and mission more fully?

• How do I answer the question of Jesus, "Who do you say I am?" Does my answer demonstrate a growth in my faith in recent years?

• Why did Peter rebuke Jesus and why did Jesus speak so harshly to Peter?

Prayer

Jesus, I believe that you are the Messiah, the Son of the living God. I thank you for the gift of my faith, and I ask that you reveal to me a deeper understanding and practical implications of this faith each day.

Jesus took with him Peter, James and his brother John and led them up a high mountain, by themselves. And he was transfigured before them. Matt 17:1–2

Mount Tabor: Church of the Transfiguration

MATTHEW 17:1–9 *¹Six days later, Jesus took with him Peter and James and his brother John and led them up a high mountain, by themselves. ²And he was transfigured before them, and his face shone like the sun, and his clothes became dazzling white. ³Suddenly there appeared to them Moses and Elijah, talking with him. ⁴Then Peter said to Jesus, "Lord, it is good for us to be here; if you wish, I will make three dwellings here, one for you, one for Moses, and one for Elijah." ⁵While he was still speaking, suddenly a bright cloud overshadowed them, and from the cloud a voice said, "This is my Son, the Beloved; with him I am well pleased; listen to him!" ⁶When the disciples heard this, they fell to the ground and were overcome by fear. ⁷But Jesus came and touched them, saying, "Get up and do not be afraid." ⁸And when they looked up, they saw no one except Jesus himself alone. ⁹As they were coming down the mountain, Jesus ordered them, "Tell no one about the vision until after the Son of Man has been raised from the dead."*

The Gospel account does not name the "high mountain" on which the transfiguration of Jesus took place, but an early tradition named Mount Tabor as the site. This Mount of the Transfiguration rises majestically from the Plain of Esdraelon south of the hills of Galilee. It is circular and almost perfect in its symmetry. From its top, where it flattens off, the whole of central Galilee can be viewed below.

In the fourth century a basilica was built here, and a sixth-century pilgrim reported three basilicas there, honoring Moses, Elijah, and Jesus. Today's Basilica of the Transfiguration incorporates some of the ancient elements. On the right and left of the entrance are two older chapels, one dedicated to Elijah, the other to Moses. The upper level of the church is dominated by a glowing mosaic of the transfiguration. The lower level contains remains of the Byzantine church and is marked by a window of a peacock, a traditional symbol of the resurrection.

The gospel speaks about a wondrous change in Jesus' appearance on the high mountain. The dazzling garments of Jesus and his glowing face are an expression of divinity, of the glory of God's Son (verse 2). Moses and Elijah, ancient figures representing God's revelation in the Old Testament, appear with Jesus (verse 3). Peter, filled with awe and reverence, wanted to keep this experience forever and suggested that he erect three tents for them (verse 4). The voice of God identifies Jesus as his Son and asks that his disciples "listen to him" (verse 5).

In Eastern Christian spirituality, the transfiguration expresses the belief that God wants to transform us all into his own divine likeness. In the transfiguration we experience a person totally possessed by God, completely on fire with God, perfectly reflecting the divine image. This divinization is what our transforming God would do if he were truly given free rein in our lives. We have all had glimpses this experience: when we touch God personally in deep prayer, when our hearts are lifted listening to glorious music, when awesome worship fills our spirits with holiness.

The account of the transfiguration occurs in the gospel immediately after Jesus first prophesies his death and begins his journey toward Jerusalem. This is a reminder to us that transforming experiences of God's presence are never given to us simply to be enjoyed for their own sake. The gift is given within the context of our vocation, to strengthen us for God's calling—a calling that, for the Christian, always includes the call to take up the cross.

Reflection and discussion

• What gives me hope when my faith is weak and challenged by discouragement?

• Why is it significant that Moses and Elijah appeared with Jesus on the mountain?

• When was the last time—if ever—I had a transforming experience of the presence of God?

• Is it time for me to do some mountain-climbing with Jesus?

Prayer

Lord, I often get discouraged and stop trusting in you. Give me glimpses of your glory in the midst of my ordinary life. Help me to trust in your power and hope in the future.

Jacob's will was there, and Jesus, tired out by his journey, was sitting by the well. It was about noon. John 4:6

Shechem: Jacob's Well

JOHN 4:3–26 *³[Jesus] left Judea and started back to Galilee. ⁴But he had to go through Samaria. ⁵So he came to a Samaritan city called Sychar, near the plot of ground that Jacob had given to his son Joseph. ⁶Jacob's well was there, and Jesus, tired out by his journey, was sitting by the well. It was about noon.*

⁷A Samaritan woman came to draw water, and Jesus said to her, "Give me a drink." ⁸(His disciples had gone to the city to buy food.) ⁹The Samaritan woman said to him, "How is it that you, a Jew, ask a drink of me, a woman of Samaria?" (Jews do not share things in common with Samaritans.) ¹⁰Jesus answered her, "If you knew the gift of God, and who it is that is saying to you, 'Give me a drink,' you would have asked him, and he would have given you living water." ¹¹The woman said to him, "Sir, you have no bucket, and the well is deep. Where do you get that living water? ¹²Are you greater than our ancestor Jacob, who gave us the well, and with his sons and his flocks drank from it?" ¹³Jesus said to her, "Everyone who drinks of this water will be thirsty again, ¹⁴but those who drink of the water that I will give them will never be thirsty. The water that I will give will become in them a spring of water gushing up to eternal life." ¹⁵The woman said to him, "Sir, give me this water, so that I may never be thirsty or have to keep coming here to draw water."

¹⁶*Jesus said to her, "Go, call your husband, and come back."* ¹⁷*The woman answered him, "I have no husband." Jesus said to her, "You are right in saying, "I have no husband";* ¹⁸*for you have had five husbands, and the one you have now is not your husband. What you have said is true!"* ¹⁹*The woman said to him, "Sir, I see that you are a prophet.* ²⁰*Our ancestors worshiped on this mountain, but you say that the place where people must worship is in Jerusalem."* ²¹*Jesus said to her, "Woman, believe me, the hour is coming when you will worship the Father neither on this mountain nor in Jerusalem.* ²²*You worship what you do not know; we worship what we know, for salvation is from the Jews.* ²³*But the hour is coming, and is now here, when the true worshippers will worship the Father in spirit and truth, for the Father seeks such as these to worship him.* ²⁴*God is spirit, and those who worship him must worship in spirit and truth."* ²⁵*The woman said to him, "I know that Messiah is coming" (who is called Christ). "When he comes, he will proclaim all things to us."* ²⁶*Jesus said to her, "I am he, the one who is speaking to you."*

Between Galilee and Judea lies the region of Samaria. The ancient town of Shechem lay in a valley between Mount Ebal and Mount Gerizim (see Joshua 8:33). Though related to the Jews, the Samaritans were regarded as non-Jews and were shunned by the Jewish people. After the Assyrians invaded the northern kingdom of Israel in the eighth century B.C., they brought foreign people into the land who intermarried with the remaining Israelites. The Judeans shunned the Samaritans and considered them unfaithful to God's law, mixing Israelite religion with pagan elements. In the fourth century B.C. the Samaritans built their own temple on Mount Gerizim to rival that in Jerusalem (verse 20).

Most Jews would travel from Galilee to Jerusalem along the Jordan River valley to avoid passing through Samaria. But Jesus passed through Samaria (verse 4) and stopped to drink at Jacob's well (verse 6). Today the well, thought to be dug by Jacob, son of Isaac, is enclosed by an Orthodox church. The church is incomplete, with walls but no roof. It stands on the ruins of a fourth-century church that was built in the shape of a cross. The well of Jacob was in the crypt beneath the altar, and today can be found down a flight of steps in a small chapel adorned with candles and icons. The water is still fresh and good for drinking. It is drawn up in a bucket from the deep well. It is "living water"—water that flows from springs within the earth—as contrasted with water gathered from rainfall into cisterns.

The well was the center of communal life for the ancient people of the Bible. It tapped into ground water, and so in the dry summers was their source of life sustaining water. It was also a gathering place, a place where people met for conversation and laughter. It was even a place where love began; it was at a well that Isaac found his wife Rebecca (Gen 24). So when Jesus meets the Samaritan woman at the well of Jacob, we should be prepared for an encounter filled with profound possibility.

The woman is shocked that Jesus, a Jew, was speaking to her, a Samaritan. The woman came to the well at noon, in the heat of the day, to avoid the other women of the town. But Jesus invited her to experience forgiveness and new life. Despite her sins, he offers her the true living water, a sharing in God's life through his Spirit. Jesus compares this life to an internal "spring of water gushing up to eternal life" (verse 14).

Realizing by now that Jesus was more than a casual visitor, the woman thought this Jewish prophet might have some new insight into the ancient controversy between Jews and Samaritans as to where the true temple should be located. Jesus replied that the time is coming when believers would worship God neither on Mount Gerizim nor in Jerusalem. The place of worship will be relatively unimportant in the new relationship with God that he offers. The new temple for all people will be the body of the risen Lord (John 2:19–21), in which people will worship in spirit and truth (verse 24). Realizing that Jesus may indeed be the long-awaited Messiah, the woman immediately left her water jar and went into the Samaritan town to spread the good news of Jesus.

In his earthly ministry Jesus continually broke down the barriers that divided people from one another. The visit of Jesus to Samaria sowed the seeds of evangelization which would bring early Christian missionaries into Samaria and then to all the world (Acts 1:8).

Reflection and discussion

•What was so surprising about Jesus' encounter with the Samaritan woman?

• What are the barriers that I erect between myself and other people?

• How can I imitate Jesus in breaking down the barriers that divide people from one another?

Prayer

Source of Living Water, you are the source of refreshing life for all people. Help me to realize my thirst for you and for the new life you offer me. Quench my thirst with the gift of your Spirit and renew the grace of Baptism within me.

**Jesus entered Jericho and was passing through it.
A man was there named Zacchaeus.** Luke 19:1

Jericho

LUKE 18:35—19:10 ³⁵ *As he approached Jericho, a blind man was sitting by the roadside begging.* ³⁶ *When he heard a crowd going by, he asked what was happening.* ³⁷ *They told him, "Jesus of Nazareth is passing by."* ³⁸ *Then he shouted, "Jesus, Son of David, have mercy on me!"* ³⁹ *Those who were in front sternly ordered him to be quiet; but he shouted even more loudly, "Son of David, have mercy on me!"* ⁴⁰ *Jesus stood still and ordered the man to be brought to him; and when he came near, he asked him,* ⁴¹ *"What do you want me to do for you?" He said, "Lord, let me see again."* ⁴² *Jesus said to him, "Receive your sight; your faith has saved you."* ⁴³ *Immediately he regained his sight and followed him, glorifying God; and all the people, when they saw it, praised God.*

¹ *He entered Jericho and was passing through it.* ² *A man was there named Zacchaeus; he was a chief tax collector and was rich.* ³ *He was trying to see who Jesus was, but on account of the crowd he could not, because he was short in stature.* ⁴ *So he ran ahead and climbed a sycamore tree to see him, because he was going to pass that way.* ⁵ *When Jesus came to the place, he looked up and said to him, "Zacchaeus, hurry and come down; for I must stay at your house today."* ⁶ *So he hurried down and was happy to welcome him.* ⁷ *All who saw it began to*

grumble and said, "He has gone to be the guest of one who is a sinner." ⁸Zacchaeus stood there and said to the Lord, "Look, half of my possessions, Lord, I will give to the poor; and if I have defrauded anyone of anything, I will pay back four times as much." ⁹Then Jesus said to him, "Today salvation has come to this house, because he too is a son of Abraham. ¹⁰For the Son of Man came to seek out and to save the lost."

Jericho is a pretty town in the Jordan valley. It was called the "city of palm trees" in the Old Testament. The modern town is still characterized by its date palms, fruits, and vegetables. Near present-day Jericho is ancient Jericho, a hill under which archaeologists have uncovered at least fifteen layers of cities and towns dating back to 7000 B.C. The Israelites took the town from its Canaanite inhabitants during the period of Israel's conquest (Josh 6). Nearby are the remains of the Jericho built by Herod the Great. Here are ruins of palaces, a theater, and hippodrome. Because of its mild climate, Jericho became a winter resort for Jewish aristocracy.

When traveling from Galilee to Jerusalem, Jesus most often went south along the Jordan River valley until reaching Jericho, then he turned westward and began the steep ascent to Jerusalem. As Jesus approached Jericho, a blind man heard that Jesus was coming and shouted out, "Son of David, have pity on me!" (verse 39). The last "son of David" on the throne of Judah had been King Zedekiah. The Babylonians captured him near Jericho and blinded him before bringing him into exile (2 Kings 25:5–7). His disobedience had lost him his sight and his kingdom. Jesus, the new Son of David, gave sight to the blind man and offered him a share in the kingdom of God. This is the gift that Jesus offers to us all: the ability to see the world with new eyes, to participate in the new life of God's kingdom.

The heart of Jesus' ministry was "to seek out and to save the lost" (verse 10). As the chief tax collector of Jericho, Zacchaeus was probably the most hated man in the region. Though wealthy and powerful, he was not happy. In the character of Zacchaeus Jesus saw a man trapped in his own failure, desperately trying to be something better. Urged on by the courage of desperation, the enterprising Zacchaeus climbed the sycamore tree and Jesus invited him to share in his life.

Zacchaeus changed his life upon meeting Jesus, and as evidence of his change he promised to restore his ill-gotten gains fourfold and to give half his goods to the poor (verse 8). The disposition of the heart is symbolized by the disposition of possessions. Zacchaeus turned his life around; he experienced the kind of repentance and personal transformation that gives hope to us all.

Pilgrims to Jericho are shown a sycamore tree which local residents say Zacchaeus climbed. The tree is only for imaginative effect since the Jericho of Jesus' times would have been nearer to the ancient archaeological site. But the sycamore tree reminds us of the energetic enthusiasm of Zacchaeus and inspires us to overcome whatever obstacles prevent us from seeing and welcoming Jesus.

Reflection and discussion

• What blind spot or obstacle prevents me from seeing Jesus? What can I do about it?

• What in the character of Zacchaeus would I like to imitate?

• In what way has Jesus taken the initiative and invited himself into my house (verse 5)?

Prayer

Son of David, have pity on me. You know my blindness, frailties, and failures. Heal those parts of me that are weak and give me a restless enthusiasm to seek and follow you.

Bethany was near Jerusalem, some two miles away, and many of the Jews had come to Martha and Mary to console them about their brother. John 11:18-19

Bethany: The Tomb of Lazarus

JOHN 11:32–44 ³²*When Mary came where Jesus was and saw him, she knelt at his feet and said to him, "Lord, if you had been here, my brother would not have died." ³³When Jesus saw her weeping, and the Jews who came with her also weeping, he was greatly disturbed in spirit and deeply moved. ³⁴He said, "Where have you laid him?" They said to him, "Lord, come and see." ³⁵Jesus began to weep. ³⁶So the Jews said, "See how he loved him!" ³⁷But some of them said, "Could not he who opened the eyes of the blind man have kept this man from dying?"*

³⁸Then Jesus, again greatly disturbed, came to the tomb. It was a cave, and a stone was lying against it. ³⁹Jesus said, "Take away the stone." Martha, the sister of the dead man, said to him, "Lord, already there is a stench because he has been dead for four days." ⁴⁰Jesus said to her, "Did I not tell you that if you believed, you would see the glory of God?" ⁴¹So they took away the stone. And Jesus looked upwards and said, "Father, I thank you for having heard me. ⁴²I knew that you always hear me, but I have said this for the sake of the crowd standing here, so that they may believe that you sent me." ⁴³When he had said this, he cried with a loud voice, "Lazarus, come out!" ⁴⁴The dead man came out, his hands and feet bound with strips of cloth, and his face wrapped in a cloth. Jesus said to them, "Unbind him, and let him go."

JOHN 12:1–11

¹*Six days before the Passover Jesus came to Bethany, the home of Lazarus, whom he had raised from the dead.* ²*There they gave a dinner for him. Martha served, and Lazarus was one of those at the table with him.* ³*Mary took a pound of costly perfume made of pure nard, anointed Jesus' feet, and wiped them with her hair. The house was filled with the fragrance of the perfume.* ⁴*But Judas Iscariot, one of his disciples (the one who was about to betray him), said,* ⁵*"Why was this perfume not sold for three hundred denarii and the money given to the poor?"* ⁶*(He said this not because he cared about the poor, but because he was a thief; he kept the common purse and used to steal what was put into it.)* ⁷*Jesus said, "Leave her alone. She bought it so that she might keep it for the day of my burial.* ⁸*You always have the poor with you, but you do not always have me."*

⁹*When the great crowd of the Jews learned that he was there, they came not only because of Jesus but also to see Lazarus, whom he had raised from the dead.* ¹⁰*So the chief priests planned to put Lazarus to death as well,* ¹¹*since it was on account of him that many of the Jews were deserting and were believing in Jesus.*

Just over the top of the Mount of Olives, on its eastern slope, is the town of Bethany. John's gospel tells us that it is about fifteen *stades* (two miles) from Jerusalem (verse 18). It is the village where Martha, Mary, and their brother Lazarus lived. Jesus was a dear friend to this family. He would often spend his days teaching in Jerusalem, then retire for the evening to Bethany.

The tomb of Lazarus has been honored here from at least the fourth century. An early pilgrim to the Holy Land, Egeria, wrote that the church met here on the Saturday before Palm Sunday for Lazarus Day. Both Byzantine and Crusader churches formerly covered the sight. Today the tomb is connected to a mosque, but can be reached from an entrance on the street by descending twenty-four steps.

The Church of Lazarus is next to the tomb. The interior of the church is grey, reminiscent of the tomb. The three frescoes in the church commemorates the three events from the gospels that are set in Bethany. The first is the gracious hospitality of Martha and Mary when Jesus entered their village (Luke 10:38). Martha was busy with the domestic details while Mary sat at the feet of Jesus and listen to him, learning to be a disciple by listening, literally, "to his word." Jesus praises Mary for setting aside her culturally expected role and doing the one thing necessary for true hospitality—attention to the guest

(Luke 10:42). Listening attentively to the word of the Lord is the way of true discipleship and life's most necessary task.

The second event is the raising of Lazarus from the dead. The account is a powerful statement of both the humanity and divinity of Jesus. Jesus clearly loved Lazarus, and he wept at the news of his death (John 11:35–36). Yet, Jesus, "the resurrection and the life" (John 11:25), called Lazarus to come forth from the tomb (John 11:43–44). The power of Jesus to give life to Lazarus gives us the firm assurance that Jesus also has the power to transform our mortal bodies and to give us life that lasts forever. Jesus will save us from death, not by eliminating it, but by overcoming it with the gift of his life.

The final event recalled in Bethany is Mary's anointing of the feet of Jesus (John 12:3). Passover was near and Jesus was particularly grateful for the hospitality of Martha, Mary, and Lazarus at this time. Finding lodging in Jerusalem would have been difficult because of the many pilgrims coming for the feast. Martha responds to Jesus with the practical service of providing the meal while Mary responds with impractical extravagance by pouring costly perfumed oil over his feet and drying his feet with her hair.

The normal use of such perfume dictated that it be applied a few drops at a time. To use a pound at once was irrational and, in the eyes of many, foolish. No wonder the house was filled with the fragrance. But the extravagant scene represents in miniature what Jesus will do in the final days of his life. His love is lavish. He will pour out his lifeblood to anoint us with grace. His action seemed foolish to many, but the fragrance of his divine love filled the whole world.

Reflection and discussion

• What does the brief verse, "Jesus began to weep" (11:35), tell me about Jesus?

• What aspect of Mary's discipleship would I most like to imitate?

• What part of the scene of Lazarus' raising gives me the most comfort and hope?

• What would happen if I lived and loved extravagantly like Mary?

Prayer

Lord of Life, you wept at the death of Lazarus, your friend. Help me to trust in you when I consider my own inevitable death and the death of those I love. May my singular attention to your word give me comfort and hope.

SUGGESTIONS FOR FACILITATORS, GROUP SESSION 4

1. Welcome group members and ask if anyone has any questions, announcements, or requests.

2. You may want to pray this prayer as a group:
Jesus, we have walked with you from the heights of Galilee, through Samaria, and into Judea. We have traveled from the Sea of Galilee, to the mountaintop, and through the wilderness toward Jerusalem. The variety of scenery is a metaphor for the diverse landscapes of our life's pilgrimage. You lead us along treacherous, peaceful, dangerous, and protected paths. Through our many hopes and fears, protect us from harm and bring us to the new Jerusalem, where you live and reign, now and forever.

3. Ask one or more of the following questions:
  • What is the most difficult part of this study for you?
  • What did you learn about yourself this week?

4. Discuss lessons 13 through 18. Choose one or more of the questions for reflection and discussion from each lesson to talk over as a group. You may want to ask group members which question was most challenging or helpful to them as you review each lesson.

5. Keep the discussion moving, but allow time for the questions that provoke the most discussion. Encourage the group members to use "I" language in their responses.

6. After talking over each lesson, instruct group members to complete lessons 19 through 24 on their own during the six days before the next group meeting. They should write out their own answers to the questions as preparation for next week's session.

7. Ask the group what encouragement they need for the coming week. Ask members to pray for the needs of one another during the week.

8. Conclude by praying aloud together the prayer at the end of one of the lessons discussed. You may choose to conclude the prayer by asking members to pray aloud any requests they may have.

Map of Jerusalem at Holy Week

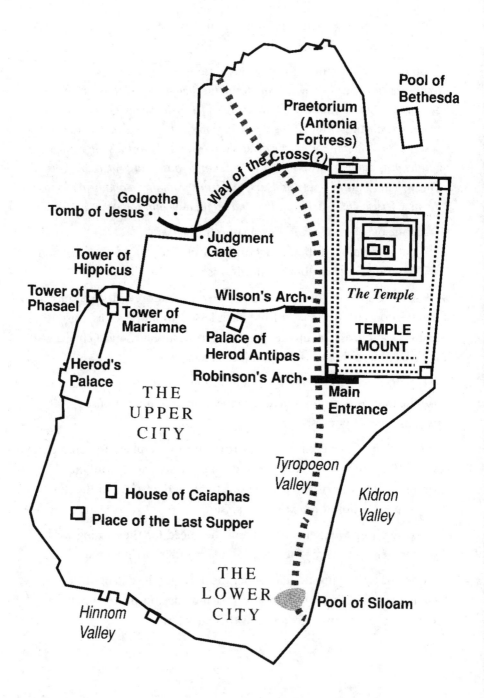

In Jerusalem by the Sheep Gate there is a pool, called in Hebrew Bethesda, which has five porticoes. In these lay many invalids —blind, lame, and paralyzed. John 5:2

Jerusalem: The Pool of Bethesda

JOHN 5:1–18 ¹*After this there was a festival of the Jews, and Jesus went up to Jerusalem.* ²*Now in Jerusalem by the Sheep Gate there is a pool, called in Hebrew Beth-zatha, which has five porticoes.* ³*In these lay many invalids—blind, lame, and paralyzed.* ⁵*One man was there who had been ill for thirty-eight years.* ⁶*When Jesus saw him lying there and knew that he had been there a long time, he said to him, "Do you want to be made well?"* ⁷*The sick man answered him, "Sir, I have no one to put me into the pool when the water is stirred up; and while I am making my way, someone else steps down ahead of me."* ⁸*Jesus said to him, "Stand up, take your mat and walk."* ⁹*At once the man was made well, and he took up his mat and began to walk. Now that day was a sabbath.* ¹⁰*So the Jews said to the man who had been cured, "It is the sabbath; it is not lawful for you to carry your mat."* ¹¹*But he answered them, "The man who made me well said to me, 'Take up your mat and walk.'"* ¹²*They asked him, "Who is the man who said to you, 'Take it up and walk'?"* ¹³*Now the man who had been healed did not know who it was, for Jesus had disappeared in the crowd that was there.* ¹⁴*Later Jesus found him in the temple and said to him, "See, you have been made well! Do not sin any more, so that nothing worse happens to you."* ¹⁵*The man went* *away and told the Jews that it was Jesus who had made him well.* [16]*Therefore the Jews started persecuting Jesus, because he was doing such things on the sabbath.* [17]*But Jesus answered them, "My Father is still working, and I also am working."* [18]*For this reason the Jews were seeking all the more to kill him, because he was not only breaking the sabbath, but was also calling God his own Father, thereby making himself equal to God.*

I n the time of Jesus the Pool of Bethesda (sometimes called Beth-zatha) was just north of the temple, near the gate where the sheep were sold and brought in to be sacrificed. The pool was surrounded by colonnaded walk-ways on its four sides, with a fifth colonnade across its middle, dividing the pool in two. This explains the gospel reference to the "five porticoes" (verse 2).

The pools were two reservoirs, filled with spring waters. Originally they served the temple whose sacrificial rites required large amounts of water to preserve the cleanliness of the site. In the days of Jesus, the waters were thought to have curative powers at certain times of the day when the inter-mittent springs bubbled up into the pools. The sick, blind, and lame would sit or lie along the five porticoes (verse 3); and when the waters stirred they would try to enter the waters to be cured (verse 7).

A verse was added to the gospel in the second century explaining the belief of some of the Jews of Jesus' day: "For an angel of the Lord went down at cer-tain seasons into the pool, and stirred up the water; whoever stepped in first after the stirring of the water was made well from whatever disease that per-son had" (verse 4). When Jesus asked the man if he wanted to be cured, the man gave the excuse, "I have no one to put me into the pool when the water is stirred up" (verse 7). He thought that Jesus would help him into the waters; by himself he could never reach the water in time, for he said, "While I am making my way, someone else steps down ahead of me."

Jesus cured the man immediately with his powerful word; he told the man to pick up his mat and walk (verse 8). But Jesus does not want us to focus on wonders alone; he followed the physical cure with spiritual encouragement (verse 14). Throughout the gospels, miracles are often invitations to a more total restoration. Jesus wants a complete healing for us, an end to any sickness that separates us from God.

After the time of Jesus, the Pool of Bethesda was enshrined as a place of healing by the Romans, who built a temple to Asclepius, the god of healing, on the site. God heals in many ways, through many means. He is the ultimate source of healing, regardless of his instruments: the medical profession, intercessory prayer, psychological or physical therapy, or shrines and miracles. For those who are afflicted, Jesus and his Holy Spirit "become in them a spring of water gushing up to eternal life" (John 4:14).

Reflection and discussion

• What is the difference between a physical cure and complete healing?

• In what ways have I experienced God's healing power?

• Do I believe that Jesus can heal the spiritual illnesses that separate me from God? Am I willing to ask for that healing?

Prayer

Lord Jesus, you desire me to be completely restored to life in its fullness. Reach into those areas of my life which are broken and failing, and speak your powerful word of healing.

They came to Jerusalem. And Jesus entered the temple and began to drive out those who were selling and those who were buying in the temple. Mark 11:15

Jerusalem: The Temple Mount and Western Wall

MARK 11:1–19 *¹When they were approaching Jerusalem, at Bethphage and Bethany, near the Mount of Olives, he sent two of his disciples ²and said to them, "Go into the village ahead of you, and immediately as you enter it, you will find tied there a colt that has never been ridden; untie it and bring it. ³If anyone says to you, 'Why are you doing this?' just say this, 'The Lord needs it and will send it back here immediately.'" ⁴They went away and found a colt tied near a door, outside in the street. As they were untying it, ⁵some of the bystanders said to them, "What are you doing, untying the colt?" ⁶They told them what Jesus had said; and they allowed them to take it. ⁷Then they brought the colt to Jesus and threw their cloaks on it; and he sat on it. ⁸Many people spread their cloaks on the road, and others spread leafy branches that they had cut in the fields. ⁹Then those who went ahead and those who followed were shouting,*

> *"Hosanna!*
> *Blessed is the one who comes in the name of the Lord!*
> *¹⁰Blessed is the coming kingdom of our ancestor David!*
> *Hosanna in the highest heaven!"*
> *¹¹Then he entered Jerusalem and went into the temple; and when he had*

*looked around at everything, as it was already late, he went out to Bethany with
the twelve.*

¹²*On the following day, when they came from Bethany, he was hungry.* ¹³*Seeing
in the distance a fig tree in leaf, he went to see whether perhaps he would find
anything on it. When he came to it, he found nothing but leaves, for it was not
the season for figs.* ¹⁴*He said to it, "May no one ever eat fruit from you again."
And his disciples heard it.*

¹⁵*Then they came to Jerusalem. And he entered the temple and began to drive
out those who were selling and those who were buying in the temple, and he
overturned the tables of the money changers and the seats of those who sold
doves;* ¹⁶*and he would not allow anyone to carry anything through the temple.*
¹⁷*He was teaching and saying, "Is it not written,*

> *'My house shall be called a house of prayer for all the nations'?*
>
> *But you have made it a den of robbers."*

¹⁸*And when the chief priests and the scribes heard it, they kept looking for a
way to kill him; for they were afraid of him, because the whole crowd was spell-
bound by his teaching.* ¹⁹*And when evening came, Jesus and his disciples went out
of the city.*

The modern pilgrim can approach Jerusalem from any direction. But
from every direction, the approach is an ascent, "up to Jerusalem."
After a steep ascent from the Jordan valley, Jesus passed through
Bethany and Bethpage, and arrived at the top of the Mount of Olives. From
there he could see the panorama of the city before him.

Today the vista of Jerusalem from the Mount of Olives looks quite different than it looked in the days of Jesus. The remains of the temple platform is
dominated by the Dome of the Rock, a shrine sacred to Islam, marking the
place where Mohammed is believed to have ascended to heaven. During the
life of Jesus, this temple mount was crowned by the gleaming structure of the
temple. The temple stood as the dominant symbol of Israel's relationship
with God. Its sacrifice, rituals, and feasts were central to that tradition to
which Jesus belonged. Yet, like the prophets of Israel before him, Jesus challenged those who would pay attention only to the outward forms of worship
without making their daily lives a means to honor God.

Jesus processed toward Jerusalem, mounted on a donkey, to shouts of welcome and acclamation. Though he was the true Davidic king, the Messiah

came in humility to the royal city. Jesus traveled down the Mount of Olives, across the Kidron Valley, and up to the temple through the Golden Gate. From the earliest centuries, the church in Jerusalem has continued to remember the royal procession of the humble Messiah into the city of his destiny with the Palm Sunday procession.

The next day Jesus entered the temple area and began to challenge the temple system and it leaders. He quoted from the Scriptures: "My house shall be called a house of prayer for all the nations, but you have made it a den of robbers" (verse 17). Like the prophets before him, Jesus condemned the corruption of the temple through symbolic actions. Overturning the money tables and upsetting the business of those selling animals to sacrifice, Jesus proclaimed that the temple was to be open for all peoples and that sacrifice was no substitute for the work of justice.

Many events from the life of Jesus took place within the area of the temple. Since he was not a Jewish priest, Jesus would not have entered the temple itself. He could be found teaching in the open area on the temple mount and within the outer colonnades. It was within these porticoes that Jesus overturned the moneychangers and cleansed the temple.

All that remains of the great temple built by Herod is part of the foundation wall on the western side. It contains the original stones of the retaining wall for the temple mount. Jewish pilgrims from around the world come to this Western Wall to lament the destruction of the temple, to remember their history, and to pray that God continue to listen to their petitions. Christians pray here together with their Jewish brothers and sisters because of the history of salvation we share. It is the place Jesus came on pilgrimage, the place where he worshiped and frequently taught. Pilgrims today often insert prayer petitions between the stones of the Western Wall.

Reflection and discussion

• Where is my temple? In what place do I most experience the presence of God?

• In what way are Jesus' entry into Jerusalem and his cleansing of the temple symbolic actions? What did they symbolize?

• How can I make my body a temple of God's Spirit and my actions a sacrifice to the Father?

• What prayer petition would I insert between the stones of the Western Wall?

Prayer

Humble king of all nations, you are the cornerstone of the new temple of God's dwelling. Make your Church a house of prayer for all people. Help me to make all that I do a fitting form of praise to you.

As Jesus came near and saw the city, he wept over it, saying, 'If you, even you, had only recognized on this day the things that make for peace!" Luke 19:41–42

Mount of Olives: Dominus Flevit Chapel

LUKE 19:41–44 *⁴¹As he came near and saw the city, he wept over it, ⁴²saying, "If you, even you, had only recognized on this day the things that make for peace! But now they are hidden from your eyes. ⁴³Indeed, the days will come upon you, when your enemies will set up ramparts around you and surround you, and hem you in on every side. ⁴⁴They will crush you to the ground, you and your children within you, and they will not leave within you one stone upon another; because you did not recognize the time of your visitation from God."*

MATTHEW 23:37–39 *³⁷"Jerusalem, Jerusalem, the city that kills the prophets and stones those who are sent to it! How often have I desired to gather your children together as a hen gathers her brood under her wings, and you were not willing! ³⁸See, your house is left to you, desolate. ³⁹For I tell you, you will not see me again until you say, 'Blessed is the one who comes in the name of the Lord.'"*

MARK 11:12–14 *¹²On the following day, when they came from Bethany, he was hungry. ¹³Seeing in the distance a fig tree in leaf, he went to see whether perhaps he would find anything on it. When he came to it, he found nothing but* *leaves, for it was not the season for figs.* ¹⁴*He said to it, "May no one ever eat fruit from you again." And his disciples heard it.*

The small chapel called Dominus Flevit (Latin for "The Lord Wept") is midway down the slope of the Mount of Olives. It was built to recall the lament of Jesus over Jerusalem, the city of peace. Jesus loved this city and its temple as his own, but he knew that it was bringing destruction upon itself because of its refusal to listen and obey its God. The words of Jesus echo those of Isaiah, Jeremiah, and the other prophets down through the centuries who warned Jerusalem's inhabitants of destruction and pleaded for their repentance. According to Luke's account, Jesus wept as he saw the city (Luke 19:41), just as many other leaders and prophets before him had wept over Jerusalem's destruction (see Neh 1:4; Jer 9:1).

The chapel is shaped in the form of a tear, and from its interior window can be seen a wondrous view of the walled city and its temple mount. In the days of Jesus, the temple towered over the walls of the city. It was Israel's great symbol of God's presence, the place where the ancient covenant was renewed each day through praise and sacrifice, the place where God's glory dwelt and where God's name was honored. But Jesus knew that his efforts to bring about repentance and forgiveness for God's people would end in his own death. He knew further that this city of peace would not know peace because it could not recognize the call to return to God.

Setting up ramparts, hemming in on every side, crushing to the ground, and not leaving one stone upon another (Luke 19:43–44)—all of these refer to the destruction of Jerusalem at the hands of the Romans which occurred forty years after Jesus' utterance. Like the prophets who warned Jerusalem of its destruction by the Babylonians in the sixth century B.C., Jesus portends the imminent destruction of the city of peace.

Each of the gospels express Jesus' lament over the city differently. In Matthew's gospel Jesus expresses the deep desire to enfold the city in his arms, "as a hen gathers her brood under her wings" (Matt 23:37). But "the city that kills the prophets and stones those who are sent to it" would not let him. In Mark's gospel, Jesus pauses to curse a fig tree, an Old Testament symbol of Israel, for its lack of fruit (Mark 11:13–14). Like the unproductive tree, Jerusalem would meet its fate because of its failure to bear fruit.

Reflection and discussion

• Can I imagine Jesus weeping over my city and my world? For what reasons would Jesus weep and lament today?

• What are "the things that make for peace" (Luke 19:42) that we must recognize? What can I do to work for peace?

• What gives me hope for the world and its future?

Prayer

Lord of the future, as you wept over Jerusalem you expressed a profound understanding of human sin. Teach me to work for peace and to place my hope in the new and eternal Jerusalem where every tear will be wiped away.

Jesus was praying in a certain place, and after he had finished,
one of his disciples said to him, "Lord, teach us to pray." Luke 11:1

Mount of Olives: Eleona Church

MARK 13:1–13, 24–27, 32–37 ¹*As he came out of the temple, one of his disciples said to him, "Look, Teacher, what large stones and what large buildings!" ²Then Jesus asked him, "Do you see these great buildings? Not one stone will be left here upon another; all will be thrown down."*

³*When he was sitting on the Mount of Olives opposite the temple, Peter, James, John, and Andrew asked him privately,* ⁴*"Tell us, when will this be, and what will be the sign that all these things are about to be accomplished?" ⁵Then Jesus began to say to them, "Beware that no one leads you astray. ⁶Many will come in my name and say, 'I am he!' and they will lead many astray. ⁷When you hear of wars and rumors of wars, do not be alarmed; this must take place, but the end is still to come. ⁸For nation will rise against nation, and kingdom against kingdom; there will be earthquakes in various places; there will be famines. This is but the beginning of the birthpangs.*

⁹*"As for yourselves, beware; for they will hand you over to councils; and you will be beaten in synagogues; and you will stand before governors and kings because of me, as a testimony to them. ¹⁰And the good news must first be proclaimed to all nations. ¹¹When they bring you to trial and hand you over, do not*

worry beforehand about what you are to say; but say whatever is given you at that time, for it is not you who speak, but the Holy Spirit. [12]*Brother will betray brother to death, and a father his child, and children will rise against parents and have them put to death;* [13]*and you will be hated by all because of my name. But the one who endures to the end will be saved.*

[24]*"But in those days, after that suffering,*
   the sun will be darkened,
   and the moon will not give its light,
[25]*and the stars will be falling from heaven,*
   and the powers in the heavens will be shaken.
[26]*Then they will see 'the Son of Man coming in clouds' with great power and glory.* [27]*Then he will send out the angels, and gather his elect from the four winds, from the ends of the earth to the ends of heaven.*

[32]*"But about that day or hour no one knows, neither the angels in heaven, nor the Son, but only the Father.* [33]*Beware, keep alert; for you do not know when the time will come.* [34]*It is like a man going on a journey, when he leaves home and puts his slaves in charge, each with his work, and commands the doorkeeper to be on the watch.* [35]*Therefore, keep awake—for you do not know when the master of the house will come, in the evening, or at midnight, or at cockcrow, or at dawn,* [36]*or else he may find you asleep when he comes suddenly.* [37]*And what I say to you I say to all: Keep awake."*

When we look today at the enormous foundation stones that remain from the foundation walls of the temple mount, we can imagine what a magnificent structure the temple must have been and why the Galilean disciples of Jesus looked back in awe as they left the temple mount (verse 1). Jesus walked up the Mount of Olives with the core group of his disciples, the two pairs of brothers (verse 3), and halted at the grotto of Eleona (Greek for "olive grove"). In this cave at the top of the Mount of Olives Jesus instructed his disciples about the destruction of Jerusalem and future events.

The Eleona grotto was one of three caves preserved by the memory of the early Christians. The other two are the cave of Christ's birth in Bethlehem and his burial sepulcher near Golgotha. In the early fourth century, Bishop Eusebius of Caesarea referred to the site: "The feet of the Lord stood on the Mount of Olives, at the cave shown here. There he prayed and revealed to his disciples the secrets of the end of the world and ascended there to heaven from the top of the Mount of Olives." A few years later the emperor Constantine ordered the Eleona Church to be built on the site, with the cave as its focal point. By the Middle Ages, the site was also associated with Jesus' teaching on prayer (Luke 11:1–13), and the Crusaders constructed the Pater Noster Church (which is Latin for "Our Father"). In the cloisters of the present church are plaques with the Lord's Prayer engraved in many different languages.

Chapter 13 of Mark's gospel and the parallel verses in Matthew and Luke are written in language called "apocalyptic," as in the book of Revelation. It uses mysterious language to describe the course of history, and offers a highly symbolic depiction of a climactic transformation of the world. Jesus compares the destruction of Jerusalem and the threats of wars, earthquakes, and famines to the labor pains that a woman endures in giving birth to a child (verses 7–8). The metaphor emphasizes that the coming period of testing is part of God's plan and that it will lead to the glorious return of Christ. Like the Passion of Jesus, the suffering of Christians will end in glory. Jesus also says that "the good news must first be proclaimed to all nations" (verse 10), which greatly extends the timetable of the divine plan, tempering the enthusiastic expectations and excessive speculation of many in the early church.

God's kingdom has been inaugurated by Jesus, but its fullness remains in the future. The climax of God's unfolding plan is the glorious revelation of Jesus and the vindication of these who have remained faithful (verses 26–27). The kingdom is God's to bring. The task of the disciple is to pray for the coming of the kingdom and to stay awake, alert, and ready (verses 32–37).

Reflection and discussion

• Why does Jesus tell us, his disciples, to "Keep alert," "Keep awake"?

• Why is the Our Father the world's most recited prayer?

• What do I think of when I pray "thy kingdom come"?

• In what ways does Jesus teach us to avoid excessive speculation about the end of the world?

Prayer

Glorious Son of Man, you urge me to stay awake, alert, and ready for your return. I pray for the coming of God's kingdom, that God's will be done on earth as it is in heaven. Come, Lord Jesus.

He will show you a large room upstairs, furnished and ready. Make preparations for us there. Mark 14:15

Jerusalem: The Upper Room

MARK 14:12–26 [12]*On the first day of Unleavened Bread, when the Passover lamb is sacrificed, his disciples said to him, "Where do you want us to go and make the preparations for you to eat the Passover?"* [13]*So he sent two of his disciples, saying to them, "Go into the city, and a man carrying a jar of water will meet you; follow him,* [14]*and wherever he enters, say to the owner of the house, 'The Teacher asks, Where is my guest room where I may eat the Passover with my disciples?'* [15]*He will show you a large room upstairs, furnished and ready. Make preparations for us there."* [16]*So the disciples set out and went to the city, and found everything as he had told them; and they prepared the Passover meal.* [17]*When it was evening, he came with the twelve.* [18]*And when they had taken their places and were eating, Jesus said, "Truly I tell you, one of you will betray me, one who is eating with me."* [19]*They began to be distressed and to say to him one after another, "Surely, not I?"* [20]*He said to them, "It is one of the twelve, one who is dipping bread into the bowl with me.* [21]*For the Son of Man goes as it is written of him, but woe to that one by whom the Son of Man is betrayed! It would have been better for that one not to have been born."*

[22]*While they were eating, he took a loaf of bread, and after blessing it he broke it, gave it to them, and said, "Take; this is my body."* [23]*Then he took a cup, and after giving thanks he gave it to them, and all of them drank from it.* [24]*He said to*

them, *"This is my blood of the covenant, which is poured out for many.* [25] *Truly I tell you, I will never again drink of the fruit of the vine until that day when I drink it new in the kingdom of God."*

[26] *When they had sung the hymn, they went out to the Mount of Olives.*

The "upper room" was a second story room of a Palestinian house, often used for guests. It was in such a room that Jesus celebrated the Last Supper with his disciples. A fifth-century tradition locates this upper room on Mount Zion, the western hill of Jerusalem. The upper room, sometimes called the Cenacle ("supper room"), is today an empty room, with a few indications of its former use as both a Crusader church and an Islamic mosque. Nearby is the Franciscan Church of the Cenacle where the Eucharist is celebrated.

Preparations for the Last Supper were made on the first day of the Feast of Unleavened Bread. On this day the lambs were slaughtered in the temple and brought to each home for the Passover meal that evening (verse 12). In the gospels of Matthew, Mark, and Luke, the Last Supper is clearly a Passover meal, also called the Seder. Jesus, whose faith was firmly rooted in the religious traditions of his people, came to the city of pilgrimage at the time of its greatest feast.

The owner of the upper room is not known, but this is not surprising in a culture that placed such emphasis on hospitality and where especially at Passover all families open their doors to pilgrims and strangers. These festive meals at the time of Jesus were eaten while reclining on cushions. The elaborate rituals of the meal are not detailed in the gospels, neither is the recounting of the story of Exodus. Only the parts of the Seder meal given radically new significance by Jesus are highlighted. The food of the Passover, the unleavened bread, is identified as the body of Jesus (verse 22). The ritual cup of wine is identified as the blood of Jesus, the blood of the covenant by which we enter a committed partnership with God (verse 23–24).

Those of us who return in mind and heart to the upper room week after week, to do again what Jesus did there, share in the Paschal (Passover) mystery which joins us in the new covenant. Tradition also associates this upper room with the appearance of the risen Jesus to his disciples (John 20:19–29) and the descent of the Holy Spirit at Pentecost (Acts 2). Though this room is empty today, the events that took place in this upper room continue to live at the heart of the Christian faith. What happened here is now renewed over and · over again across the world as the crucified and risen Lord gathers us as his people in the Holy Spirit.

Reflection and discussion

• In what ways did Jesus radically renew the ancient feast of Passover?

• In what ways can we better express hospitality toward pilgrims and strangers in our Eucharist?

• How does the Last Supper and Christian Eucharist express the heart of my Christian faith?

Prayer

Lord of life, you give me the gift of your body and blood. As I eat the bread of life and drink the cup of salvation, help me to experience the grace of your Passion and draw me to share in your risen life.

Jesus went with them to a place called Gethsemane; and he said to his disciples, "Sit here while I go over there and pray." He took with him Peter and the two sons of Zebedee, and began to be grieved and agitated. Matt 26:36–37

Mount of Olives: Gethsemane

MATTHEW 26:36–46 ³⁶*Then Jesus went with them to a place called Gethsemane; and he said to his disciples, "Sit here while I go over there and pray." ³⁷He took with him Peter and the two sons of Zebedee, and began to be grieved and agitated. ³⁸Then he said to them, "I am deeply grieved, even to death; remain here, and stay awake with me." ³⁹And going a little farther, he threw himself on the ground and prayed, "My Father, if it is possible, let this cup pass from me; yet not what I want but what you want." ⁴⁰Then he came to the disciples and found them sleeping; and he said to Peter, "So, could you not stay awake with me one hour? ⁴¹Stay awake and pray that you may not come into the time of trial; the spirit indeed is willing, but the flesh is weak." ⁴²Again he went away for the second time and prayed, "My Father, if this cannot pass unless I drink it, your will be done." ⁴³Again he came and found them sleeping, for their eyes were heavy. ⁴⁴So leaving them again, he went away and prayed for the third time, saying the same words. ⁴⁵Then he came to the disciples and said to them, "Are you still sleeping and taking your rest? See, the hour is at hand, and the Son of Man is betrayed into the hands of sinners. ⁴⁶Get up, let us be going. See, my betrayer is at hand."*

After celebrating the Last Supper, Jesus went with his disciples across the Kidron Valley to the foot of the Mount of Olives. He could have chosen to continue walking up the Mount of Olives, over its top, and into the desert to escape his betrayer and the soldiers seeking to arrest him. But Jesus stopped at a garden called Gethsemane where he prayed and agonized over his pending arrest and passion. Today there is a grove of olive trees there, gnarled and ancient trees which look as though they could have been the silent witnesses to Jesus' sorrowful prayer to the Father that fateful night.

Gethsemane (the name means "olive oil press") is accentuated by the haunting beauty of the Basilica of the Agony, also called the Church of All Nations. The dim interior of the church evokes the grief of that terrible night. The focus of the church is a large rock, surrounded by a metal crown of thorns. Here at this rock Jesus fell prostrate in prayer: "My Father, if it is possible, let this cup pass from me; yet not what I want but what you want" (verses 39, 42).

The narrative of the agony in the garden alternates between the emotional suffering of Jesus and his call to his disciples to be watchful, attentive, and prayerful. The struggle of Jesus was the choice between personal survival and obedience to all that the Father asked of him. The contrast is sharp between the awful struggle of Jesus and the weariness and inattentiveness of his closest followers.

The Grotto of Gethsemane, a few yards from the olive grove, commemorates the place where Jesus was betrayed by Judas and arrested by the authorities. This cave is basically unaltered since the time of Jesus, and Christian worship here dates back to at least the fourth century. All four of the gospels narrate the arrest of Jesus. Judas, knowing where to find Jesus, leads the authorities to him and betrays him. John's gospel adds that Judas knew the place, "because Jesus often met there with his disciples" (John 18:2). The disciples try to prevent the arrest of Jesus by using swords, but Jesus rejects their use of violence. In the end, all the disciples of Jesus desert him and flee at his darkest moment (Matt 26:56).

Gethsemane reminds us of the choice of Jesus to pour out his whole self for us. It encourages us not to grow weary and yield to selfish temptations. It urges us to watch and pray, for we don't know when our greatest test of faith will come. In our life's agonies, we can turn to our Father who turns the darkness into light and defeat into victory.

Reflection and discussion

• What makes the prayer of Jesus ambiguous (verse 39)? Are there times when I don't know what to pray for?

• What does the prayer of Jesus in Gethsemane teach me about prayer?

• How can I stay more watchful and trustful as I anticipate the struggles of life?

Prayer

Lord Jesus, you experienced pain, rejection, confusion, and loneliness. Be with me in my dark nights of weariness, indifference, and fear. Assure me that on the other side of the pain is God's loving consolation.

SUGGESTIONS FOR FACILITATORS, GROUP SESSION 5

1. Welcome group members and ask if anyone has any questions, announcements, or requests.

2. You may want to pray this prayer as a group:
Lord Jesus, you made the pilgrimage to Jerusalem many times during your life. Its temple and its many feasts were a great joy for you. But in your final visit to that city, you made the journey from this world back to your heavenly Father. As we reflect on the sites of your final week in the holy city, teach us how to make our lives a sacred journey to God. As we come together weighed down with the baggage of our journey, refresh and renew us with your Holy Spirit.

3. Ask one or more of the following questions:
   • In what ways have studying the places of Jesus' life helped you to understand him better?
   • Which of the places most intrigued you from this week's study?

4. Discuss lessons 19 through 24. Choose one or more of the questions for reflection and discussion from each lesson to talk over as a group.

5. Ask the group members to name one thing they have most appreciated about the way the group has worked during this Bible study. Ask group members to discuss any changes they might suggest in the way the group works in future studies.

6. Invite group members to complete lessons 25 through 30 on their own during the six days before the next meeting. They should write out their own answers to the questions as preparation for next week's session.

7. Conclude by praying aloud together the prayer at the end of one of the lessons discussed. You may want to end the prayer by asking members to voice prayers of thanksgiving.

They seized Jesus and led him away, bringing him into the high priest's house. But Peter was following at a distance. Luke 22:54

Jerusalem: St. Peter in Gallicantu

LUKE 22:54–62 ⁵⁴ *Then they seized [Jesus] and led him away, bringing him into the high priest's house. But Peter was following at a distance. ⁵⁵ When they had kindled a fire in the middle of the courtyard and sat down together, Peter sat among them. ⁵⁶ Then a servant girl, seeing him in the firelight, stared at him and said, "This man also was with him." ⁵⁷ But he denied it, saying, "Woman, I do not know him." ⁵⁸ A little later someone else, on seeing him, said, "You also are one of them." But Peter said, "Man, I am not!" ⁵⁹ Then about an hour later still another kept insisting, "Surely this man also was with him; for he is a Galilean." ⁶⁰ But Peter said, "Man, I do not know what you are talking about!" At that moment, while he was still speaking, the cock crowed. ⁶¹ The Lord turned and looked at Peter. Then Peter remembered the word of the Lord, how he had said to him, "Before the cock crows today, you will deny me three times." ⁶² And he went out and wept bitterly.*

After the arrest of Jesus in Gethsemane, he was taken to the house of the high priest, Caiaphas. Here Jesus was interrogated by Caiaphas and mocked and beaten by the guards. Peter had followed the arresting party "at a distance" and sat with them around a fire in the courtyard while Jesus was interrogated inside the house. Here Peter denied his master three times before the rooster crowed in the early morning hours.

The house of Caiaphas and Peter's denials are commemorated at the Church of St. Peter in Gallicantu, owned and maintained by the Assumptionist Fathers from France. Gallicantu means cock-crow, and today a golden rooster is mounted in the center of the church's roof. Mosaics of the life of Peter decorate the walls of the sanctuary. The church is situated at the top of a flight of old stone steps dating from the first century, the stairs which Jesus likely trod on his way to and from Gethsemane the night of his arrest.

While Jesus was on trial in the house of Caiaphas, Peter also found himself on trial. The judge was not the high priest and religious authorities of Jerusalem but a servant girl and the bystanders gathered around the fire that night. Peter's courtroom was the high priest's courtyard, where he testified that he was neither a friend nor a disciple of Jesus. In his moment of trial, Peter denied his relationship with Jesus, a bond that had been the deepest commitment of Peter's life. Though Peter had promised his fidelity to Jesus at the Last Supper—"Lord, I am ready to go with you to prison and to death!" (22:33)—he crumpled under his first significant challenge.

The crow of the rooster pierced the darkness of those early hours and startled Peter with the enormity of his denial. He recalled the words of Jesus at the supper that Peter would deny their relationship three times before the cock would crow. Peter denied Jesus three times, one denial for each failure to stay awake and pray in Gethsemane. Luke's gospel heightens the impact of the scene by mentioning that, at Peter's final denial, Jesus turned and looked straight at Peter (verse 61). Presumably the interrogation before Caiaphas had just concluded and Jesus was being led down from the chambers where he had been condemned and humiliated.

Beneath the modern church are ruins of an earlier Byzantine church as well as cellars and cisterns from the time of Jesus. One of those cisterns marks the imprisonment of Jesus during the night of his arrest. While Peter "went out and wept bitterly" (verse 62), Jesus was being locked away in a makeshift dungeon where he would spend the night in torturous loneliness. The exterior mosaic of the church depicts Jesus being lowered with rope into the pit and is captioned by a verse from the psalms: "You have put me in the depths of the Pit" (Ps 88:6). The whole of this psalm could have served as the prayer of Jesus that night.

Reflection and discussion

• In what courtrooms has my relationship with Jesus been on trial? At those moments, have I been a courageous or a cowardly disciple?

• How did the rooster crow serve as a reminder to Peter for the rest of his life? Have I had any similar reminders to transform my cockiness to vigilance and fidelity?

• What verse of Psalm 88 expresses my emotional response when I have been denied or betrayed by someone I love?

Prayer

Merciful Lord, you have offered me the privilege of being your disciple and walking the way of your Passion. Give me strength in times when I am tempted to deny you and forgiveness for my times of failure.

A great number of the people followed Jesus, and among them were women who were beating their breasts and wailing for him. Luke 23:27

Jerusalem: The Via Dolorosa

LUKE 23:18–32 ¹⁸ *Then they all shouted out together, "Away with this fellow! Release Barabbas for us!" ¹⁹(This was a man who had been put in prison for an insurrection that had taken place in the city, and for murder.) ²⁰Pilate, wanting to release Jesus, addressed them again; ²¹but they kept shouting, "Crucify, cruci-fy him!" ²²A third time he said to them, "Why, what evil has he done? I have found in him no ground for the sentence of death; I will therefore have him flogged and then release him." ²³But they kept urgently demanding with loud shouts that he should be crucified; and their voices prevailed. ²⁴So Pilate gave his verdict that their demand should be granted. ²⁵He released the man they asked for, the one who had been put in prison for insurrection and murder, and he handed Jesus over as they wished.*

²⁶As they led him away, they seized a man, Simon of Cyrene, who was coming from the country, and they laid the cross on him, and made him carry it behind Jesus. ²⁷A great number of the people followed him, and among them were women who were beating their breasts and wailing for him. ²⁸But Jesus turned to them and said, "Daughters of Jerusalem, do not weep for me, but weep for your-selves and for your children. ²⁹For the days are surely coming when they will say,

'Blessed are the barren, and the wombs that never bore, and the breasts that never nursed.' [30] Then they will begin to say to the mountains, 'Fall on us'; and to the hills, 'Cover us.' [31] For if they do this when the wood is green, what will happen when it is dry?"

[32] Two others also, who were criminals, were led away to be put to death with him.

The Via Dolorosa or Way of the Cross developed from the desire of early Christians to follow in the footsteps of Jesus on his way to crucifixion. In fourth century Jerusalem, Christians processed with candles from Gethsemane to Calvary before dawn on Good Friday. The stations of the cross developed gradually as a popular devotion among European Christians. Some of the stations are explicitly from the biblical accounts of the passion, others are derived from popular traditions and attempts to fill in the details not mentioned in the texts. By the sixteenth century a way of the cross with fourteen stations was popular.

The Via Dolorosa in Jerusalem assumes that the trial of Jesus before Pilate took place in the Antonia Fortress that was north of the temple area. The Antonia Fortress was a massive bastion which served as the headquarters of the Roman garrison. Some scholars now hold that the trial took place further to the west at the present day Citadel. The first station is prayed on the present site of the Antonia Fortress, marked by two Franciscan chapels. The somber Chapel of the Condemnation marks Pilate's sentence that Jesus be crucified. The Chapel of the Flagellation commemorates Jesus' torturous scourging. Stained glass windows depict the flagellation of Jesus, Pilate washing his hands, and the freeing of Barabbas.

The next stations are marked along the road leading west, and the final five stations are found within the Church of the Holy Sepulcher. Like other condemned prisoners, Jesus was forced to carry the cross, or at least its crossbeam, to his place of execution. Though the site of Golgotha is today within the present walls of Jerusalem, at the time of Jesus it was outside the city gates.

The gospels record that among the crowd was a man named Simon, a Jew from Cyrene in north Africa. The soldiers demanded that Simon carry the cross of Jesus, a testimony to the weakness of Jesus after his trials and flogging. Further along the way Jesus encountered the women of the city performing their customary rituals of mourning and lamenting for the condemned prisoners. Though he was grateful for their sympathy, Jesus focused not on his own suffering but on the tragedy these women and their children would undergo when Jerusalem is besieged and destroyed.

The Stations of the Cross are conducted by the Franciscans every Friday afternoon and are walked by other pilgrimage groups every day. In the days of Jesus the street was a busy thoroughfare, teeming with merchants and shoppers, donkeys and carts, beggars and soldiers, much like it is today. Rubbing shoulders with the life of the street is part of experiencing the Way of the Cross. It is a path that often intersects the journey of our own lives. Each of us have had, or will have, our way of the cross—down a hospital hallway to surgery, to divorce court, to the bedside of a dying spouse—and having followed the way of Jesus will give us strength and hope for our journey.

Reflection and discussion

• List the people who followed Jesus along the way of the cross. What would I have experienced had I been one of them?

• Along what sorrowful ways have I been led in recent years?

• How does following the way of the cross help prepare me to take up the cross and follow Jesus?

• Which of the fourteen stations of the cross has the most impact on me?

• Do I see the suffering Jesus in others? Have I turned my back on Jesus in the least of my brothers and sisters?

Prayer

Merciful Lord, by your wounds I am healed. In union with you; by my wounds I can heal others. Fill me with that same love for my brothers and sisters that led you to Calvary.

**Then they brought Jesus to the place called Golgotha
(which means the place of a skull).** Mark 15:22

Jerusalem: Golgotha

MARK 15:22–41 *²²Then they brought Jesus to the place called Golgotha (which means the place of a skull). ²³And they offered him wine mixed with myrrh; but he did not take it. ²⁴And they crucified him, and divided his clothes among them, casting lots to decide what each should take.*

²⁵It was nine o'clock in the morning when they crucified him. ²⁶The inscription of the charge against him read, "The King of the Jews." ²⁷And with him they crucified two bandits, one on his right and one on his left. ²⁹Those who passed by derided him, shaking their heads and saying, "Aha! You who would destroy the temple and build it in three days, ³⁰save yourself, and come down from the cross!" ³¹In the same way the chief priests, along with the scribes, were also mocking him among themselves and saying, "He saved others; he cannot save himself. ³²Let the Messiah, the King of Israel, come down from the cross now, so that we may see and believe." Those who were crucified with him also taunted him.

³³When it was noon, darkness came over the whole land until three in the afternoon. ³⁴At three o'clock Jesus cried out with a loud voice, "Eloi, Eloi, lema sabachthani?" which means, "My God, my God, why have you forsaken me?" ³⁵When some of the bystanders heard it, they said, "Listen, he is calling for

Elijah." [36] *And someone ran, filled a sponge with sour wine, put it on a stick, and gave it to him to drink, saying, "Wait, let us see whether Elijah will come to take him down." [37] Then Jesus gave a loud cry and breathed his last. [38] And the curtain of the temple was torn in two, from top to bottom. [39] Now when the centurion, who stood facing him, saw that in this way he breathed his last, he said, "Truly this man was God's Son!"*

[40] *There were also women looking on from a distance; among them were Mary Magdalene, and Mary the mother of James the younger and of Joses, and Salome. [41] These used to follow him and provided for him when he was in Galilee; and there were many other women who had come up with him to Jerusalem.*

Immediately upon entering the Basilica of the Holy Sepulcher, a steep stairway leads upward to Golgotha (in Latin, "Calvary"), the place of the crucifixion of Jesus. The altar on the right commemorates the nailing of Jesus to the cross; the altar on the left is the place where the cross of Jesus stood. Pilgrims may reach through a hole at the base of the altar to touch the top of the stone mound which was called "the Skull." The rocky formation got its name from the fact that the sides of the mound had been quarried and looked like the outline of a skull.

Here Jesus was taunted and tormented; here soldiers gambled for his clothing, and gave him vinegar to drink. Here Jesus cried out to God with a feeling of abandonment before he shouted out his final cry in torturous pain. At this abandoned rock quarry outside the north walls of ancient Jerusalem, on a cracked and defective block of stone, Jesus suffered humanity's most memorable death. Rejected by those he had ministered to, denied, betrayed, and abandoned by his closest friends, and feeling forsaken even by God, Jesus remained unconditionally loyal and demonstrated history's decisive victory of faithful love.

Mark's passion account is organized into patterns of threes: Jesus' prayer in Gethsemane is threefold; Peter denies Jesus three times; three groups mock him on the cross: those passing by, the Jewish leaders, and those crucified with him (verses 29–32). The crucifixion itself consists of three periods of three hours each: at the third hour (9:00 A.M.) Jesus was crucified, at the sixth hour (noon) darkness came over the land, and at the ninth hour (3:00 P.M.) Jesus died (verses 25, 33–34). These threesome patterns support the scholarly opinion that the passion account developed through oral proclamation and ritual reenactment within the liturgy of the early church before it was incorporated into Mark's written gospel.

As Jesus dies, the scene flashes back to the temple. The curtain separating the holy place from the holy of holies (Exod 26:31–37) was torn in two from top to bottom (verse 38). With the death of Jesus there is no longer a need for the redemptive sacrifices in the temple. Jesus fulfills the function of the temple in a decisive way. Through his ultimate sacrifice, the obstacles are removed and the way to God is opened for all humanity, Gentiles as well as Jews. Indeed, it is a Gentile centurion who declares at Jesus' death: "Truly this man was God's Son" (verse 39). Only by dying on the cross, rather than coming down from the cross as his taunters suggested, could the true identity of Jesus be understood and proclaimed.

Through the cross of Jesus, our God became credible to a suffering world by entering fully into human pain. There are no depths of human experience to which Jesus has not plunged. He shares with us the loneliness of suffering, the pain of abandonment, the darkness of depression, and the agony of death. Yet, on the cross Jesus did more than tell us he shares our pain; he transforms it with his love, bringing light out of darkness and life out of death.

Reflection and discussion

• Meditate on an image of Jesus crucified. What does the wood of the cross mean to me?

• In my opinion, are there indications today that the cross is being removed from the center of Christianity? Why or why not?

Prayer

Crucified Savior, your death on the cross brought life to the world. Help me in my suffering and be with me at the hour of my death.

Then Joseph bought a linen cloth, and taking down the body, wrapped it in the linen cloth, and laid it in a tomb that had been hewn out of the rock. Mark 15:46

Jerusalem: Basilica of the Holy Sepulcher

MARK 15:42—16:8 *⁴²When evening had come, and since it was the day of Preparation, that is, the day before the sabbath, ⁴³Joseph of Arimathea, a respected member of the council, who was also himself waiting expectantly for the kingdom of God, went boldly to Pilate and asked for the body of Jesus. ⁴⁴Then Pilate wondered if he were already dead; and summoning the centurion, he asked him whether he had been dead for some time. ⁴⁵When he learned from the centurion that he was dead, he granted the body to Joseph. ⁴⁶Then Joseph bought a linen cloth, and taking down the body, wrapped it in the linen cloth, and laid it in a tomb that had been hewn out of the rock. He then rolled a stone against the door of the tomb. ⁴⁷Mary Magdalene and Mary the mother of Joses saw where the body was laid.*

¹When the sabbath was over, Mary Magdalene, and Mary the mother of James, and Salome bought spices, so that they might go and anoint him. ²And very early on the first day of the week, when the sun had risen, they went to the tomb. ³They had been saying to one another, "Who will roll away the stone for us from the entrance to the tomb?" ⁴When they looked up, they saw that the stone, which was very large, had already been rolled back. ⁵As they entered the

tomb, they saw a young man, dressed in a white robe, sitting on the right side;
and they were alarmed. ⁶But he said to them, "Do not be alarmed; you are look-
ing for Jesus of Nazareth, who was crucified. He has been raised; he is not here.
Look, there is the place they laid him. ⁷But go, tell his disciples and Peter that he
is going ahead of you to Galilee; there you will see him, just as he told you." ⁸So
they went out and fled from the tomb, for terror and amazement had seized
them; and they said nothing to anyone, for they were afraid.

The Basilica of the Holy Sepulcher is dreary and dark, but the saving events which occurred in this place have brought light to all the earth. At the center of the rotunda, beneath the large dome, is the marble monument containing the rock-hewn tomb of Jesus. The low doorway of the monument leads to the first chamber, the chapel of the angel, and through a second doorway is the chamber containing the marble-covered stone slab on which the body of Jesus was laid to rest. Here pilgrims touch the stone, recite brief prayers, light candles, and recall the gospel event.

If we could imaginatively take down the entire basilica, with its pillars, altars, lamps, mosaics, and stone flooring, we would find a singular tomb cut away from other burial tombs in an area formerly used as a limestone quarry. In A.D. 30, the place could be described simply as a garden lying outside the walls of Jerusalem. Deserted and unprotected, it was a suitable place for the crucifixion and burial of criminals.

In the fourth century, Constantine created a magnificent basilica on this site. There he enclosed the rock of Calvary and the sacred tomb in what he described as the central shrine of Christendom. The church was damaged and restored, torched and demolished several times through the centuries and the present church is a confusing assembly of passageways and altars cared for by Armenian, Greek, and Latin Christians.

Jesus was hastily taken down from the cross, wrapped in a linen cloth, and laid in the tomb on a Friday before sundown, when the Sabbath began. His disciples would then rest on the Sabbath and return to the tomb at sunrise on Sunday, the third day, to complete the anointing of his body for burial. The proclamation "He has been raised" changed the lives of those disciples and our own lives forever.

The empty tomb is filled with awesome mystery. Here the great mystery of faith was accomplished: Christ has died, Christ is risen, Christ will come again. It is the last station of the sorrowful way of the cross, but it is the beginning of the glorious way of resurrection.

The message of the angel, "Look, there is the place they laid him," continues to call pilgrims to see the empty tomb; but the other message, "He has been raised; he is not here," assures us that the truest pilgrimage is going out to tell others the good news and living the new life given to us by our risen Lord.

Reflection and discussion

• Why is the empty tomb a cause for trembling and bewilderment as well as for joyful hope?

• What does the empty tomb teach me about the value and the futility of pilgrimage?

• In what ways can I be a witness to the resurrection of Jesus?

Prayer

Risen Lord, you never abandon your disciples and your rising assures us that your word is trustworthy. By your cross and resurrection you have set us free; you are the Savior of the world. Help me to place my hope in you and entrust my future to you.

Jesus said to them, "Bring some of the fish you have just caught." So Simon Peter went aboard and hauled the net ashore, full of large fish. John 21:10–11

Tabgha: Church of Peter's Primacy

JOHN 21:1–19 *¹After these things Jesus showed himself again to the disciples by the Sea of Tiberias; and he showed himself in this way. ²Gathered there together were Simon Peter, Thomas called the Twin, Nathanael of Cana in Galilee, the sons of Zebedee, and two others of his disciples. ³Simon Peter said to them, "I am going fishing." They said to him, "We will go with you." They went out and got into the boat, but that night they caught nothing.*

⁴Just after daybreak, Jesus stood on the beach; but the disciples did not know that it was Jesus. ⁵Jesus said to them, "Children, you have no fish, have you?" They answered him, "No." ⁶He said to them, "Cast the net to the right side of the boat, and you will find some." So they cast it, and now they were not able to haul it in because there were so many fish. ⁷That disciple whom Jesus loved said to Peter, "It is the Lord!" When Simon Peter heard that it was the Lord, he put on some clothes, for he was naked, and jumped into the sea. ⁸But the other disciples came in the boat, dragging the net full of fish, for they were not far from the land, only about a hundred yards off.

⁹When they had gone ashore, they saw a charcoal fire there, with fish on it, and bread. ¹⁰Jesus said to them, "Bring some of the fish that you have just caught." [11] *So Simon Peter went aboard and hauled the net ashore, full of large fish, a hundred fifty-three of them; and though there were so many, the net was not torn.* [12] *Jesus said to them, "Come and have breakfast." Now none of the disciples dared to ask him, "Who are you?" because they knew it was the Lord.* [13] *Jesus came and took the bread and gave it to them, and did the same with the fish.* [14] *This was now the third time that Jesus appeared to the disciples after he was raised from the dead.*

[15] *When they had finished breakfast, Jesus said to Simon Peter, "Simon son of John, do you love me more than these?" He said to him, "Yes, Lord; you know that I love you." Jesus said to him, "Feed my lambs."* [16] *A second time he said to him, "Simon son of John, do you love me?" He said to him, "Yes, Lord; you know that I love you." Jesus said to him, "Tend my sheep."* [17] *He said to him the third time, "Simon son of John, do you love me?" Peter felt hurt because he said to him the third time, "Do you love me?" And he said to him, "Lord, you know everything; you know that I love you." Jesus said to him, "Feed my sheep.* [18] *Very truly, I tell you, when you were younger, you used to fasten your own belt and to go wherever you wished. But when you grow old, you will stretch out your hands, and someone else will fasten a belt around you and take you where you do not wish to go."* [19] *(He said this to indicate the kind of death by which he would glorify God.) After this he said to him, "Follow me."*

On the shores of the Sea of Galilee is a small church commemorating the appearance of the risen Christ to his disciples as they were fishing from their boats. The chapel is built on rock and juts out into the sea. The church is called the Church of the Primacy of St. Peter since here Christ commissioned Peter to feed and tend the sheep of his flock.

The disciples had returned to Galilee after the death of Jesus, taking up again their old trade of fishing (verse 3). The risen Lord appeared to them and told them where to find a wondrously abundant catch of fish (verse 6). Peter jumped into the sea and hauled in the overflowing nets. The great catch of fish symbolically represents the apostolic mission Jesus gives to the community of his disciples. The number of fish—153—in some way emphasizes the completeness and universality of the mission. St. Jerome speculates there were 153 varieties of fish known at the time. The great catch seems to be a symbolic equivalent to the apostolic commission Jesus gives to his followers at the end of Matthew: "Go and make disciples of all the nations" (Matt 28:19).

The rock which the present church encloses is called Mensa Christi, the Table of Christ, and has been pointed out from at least the fourth century as the place where the risen Christ prepared a meal. The meal of bread and fish which Jesus cooked for his disciples on the shore represents the eucharistic communion which the risen Lord prepares for his Church.

The charcoal fire on the shore recalls the fire in the courtyard when Peter had denied Jesus (John 18:18). The three questions asked of Peter, "Do you love me?" enable Peter to face up to the memories of that shameful night. The three responses of Peter express the essence of true discipleship and reconcile Peter with his Lord. Jesus' threefold command to Peter, "feed my lambs, tend my sheep, feed my sheep" establish him as the shepherd of God's flock with the task of teaching and nourishing the flock in imitation of the Shepherd Jesus.

Outside the church, on the shore of the lake, there is a modern bronze sculpture of this encounter of Peter and Jesus. Peter is the rock of Christ's church, the fisherman of God's people, and the shepherd of the flock. Like the love of Peter, our love for Jesus must be translated into action. The words of Jesus, "Follow me" (verse 19), are addressed to us all. The journey in the footsteps of Jesus leads us always to new beginnings and new adventures in service.

Reflection and discussion

• Imagine this resurrection scene on the shores of Galilee—its sights, sounds, smells, and tastes. Which sensation has the most profound effects on me?

• In what ways does this resurrection scene symbolically express the future mission of the church?

• How did Jesus persuade Peter to acknowledge his earlier denials and be reconciled to him?

• What does the experience of Peter teach me about leadership in the way of Jesus?

• Is love for Jesus the essential foundation for my care and service of others? What is my response to Jesus' question, "Do you love me?"

Prayer

Good Shepherd, you have called your Church to bring in a great catch for your kingdom. Help me to teach, feed, and evangelize your people in the unique way you have chosen for me.

While Jesus was blessing them, he withdrew from them and was carried up into heaven. Luke 24:51

Mount of Olives: Shrine of the Ascension

LUKE 24:50–53 ⁵⁰ *Then [Jesus] led them out as far as Bethany, and, lifting up his hands, he blessed them.* ⁵¹ *While he was blessing them, he withdrew from them and was carried up into heaven.* ⁵² *And they worshiped him, and returned to Jerusalem with great joy;* ⁵³ *and they were continually in the temple blessing God.*

ACTS 1:6–12 ⁶ *So when they had come together, they asked him, "Lord, is this the time when you will restore the kingdom to Israel?"* ⁷ *He replied, "It is not for you to know the times or periods that the Father has set by his own authority.* ⁸ *But you will receive power when the Holy Spirit has come upon you; and you will be my witnesses in Jerusalem, in all Judea and Samaria, and to the ends of the earth."* ⁹ *When he had said this, as they were watching, he was lifted up, and a cloud took him out of their sight.* ¹⁰ *While he was going and they were gazing up toward heaven, suddenly two men in white robes stood by them.* ¹¹ *They said, "Men of Galilee, why do you stand looking up toward heaven? This Jesus, who has been taken up from you into heaven, will come in the same way as you saw him go into heaven."*

¹² *Then they returned to Jerusalem from the mount called Olivet, which is near Jerusalem, a sabbath day's journey away.*

The ascension of Jesus is commemorated at a circular shrine on the top of the Mount of Olives. There a rough piece of rock marks the place where an early tradition says that Jesus left this world to return to the Father. An earlier shrine of the fourth century consisted of a circular colonnade around the rock which was open to the sky. The distance between this shrine and the city of Jerusalem is "a Sabbath day's journey" (Acts 1:12), about half a mile, the maximum allowable distance a Jew could travel on the Sabbath.

The ascension represents Jesus leaving this world and entering the presence of God. It expresses the reality that Jesus is not only risen, but now reigns in power and glory with the Father. The gospel of Luke presents the resurrection and ascension as one continuous movement to the Father, making no references to time between the resurrection and ascension. The Acts of the Apostles notes that a period of forty days separated the resurrection and ascension (Acts 1:3), marking a period of transition between the ministry of Jesus and the age of the church.

Often people wonder what it would have been like to live with Jesus and follow him throughout his earthly life. But truly we are able to live more closely to Jesus now than we could have when he walked the earth. The first disciples lived *with* Jesus; but now, in his return to the Father and the sending of his Spirit, we live *in* Jesus. We too are challenged by the angels not to "stand there looking at the sky" (Acts 1:11). We are, rather, to be witnesses to Jesus Christ (1:8), in every place and to every one.

The resurrection and ascension challenge us to discover the other side of pilgrimage. Conventional pilgrimage means going somewhere else to find God in a new way; the other side of pilgrimage means going somewhere else in order to bring God in a new way to that place. The call of the risen Christ to be witnesses, not only in Jerusalem, Judea, and Samaria, but "to the ends of the earth" (Acts 1:8) convinces us that now every place in the world can be a holy land. We can discover God's presence in the least likely places, and we can bring the presence of God to places that wait in darkness for the dawning light of our Risen Lord.

Reflection and discussion

• Why am I able to live more closely to Jesus now than I could have when he walked the earth?

• What souvenir would I like to keep with me from my pilgrimage?

• In what way is the place in which I now live holy ground?

• In what way am I now prepared to discover the other side of pilgrimage?

Prayer

Lord Jesus, help me to see that all places and all people are holy because you have walked the earth. Be with me always, and encourage me to hope in your glorious return.

SUGGESTIONS FOR FACILITATORS, GROUP SESSION 6

1. Welcome group members and make any final announcements or requests.

2. You may want to pray this prayer as a group:

Jesus, you are risen, glorified, and exalted. We have journeyed to the places of your earthly life, so that we may more fully appreciate the places of our earthly life. We have followed your way of the cross, so that we may with greater courage take up our cross and follow you. We have sought out your empty tomb and the mystical places of your risen presence, so that we may realize that you are with us always. Continue to guide us along our pilgrim way and lead us home to be with you forever.

3. Ask one or more of the following questions:
   • In what way has this study challenged you the most?
   • How have you become a different person as a result of your pilgrimage in the footsteps of Jesus?

4. Discuss lessons 25 through 30. Choose one or more of the questions for reflection and discussion from each lesson to discuss as a group.

5. Ask the group if they would like to study another book in the Threshold Bible Study series. Discuss the topic and dates, and make a decision among those interested. Ask the group members to suggest people they would like to invite to participate in the next study series.

6. Ask the group to discuss the insights that stand out most from this study over the past six weeks.

7. Conclude by praying aloud the following prayer or another of your own choosing:

Holy Spirit, you are alive in our hearts as we seek to worship the Father in spirit and in truth. Bless us with the fire you your love. Continue to deepen our love for the word of God in the holy Scriptures and draw us more deeply into the heart of Jesus. Guide us and empower us as we follow in the footsteps of Jesus along the pilgrim road of life. And when our journey is over, lead us into the glories of God's eternal kingdom where Jesus reigns as Lord of heaven and earth.

Ordering Additional Studies

Upcoming and available Threshold titles

People of the Passion

Pilgrimage in the Footsteps of Jesus

Advent Light

The Names of Jesus

The Tragic and Triumphant Cross

Jerusalem, the Holy City

The Angels of God

The Resurrection and the Life

The Mysteries of the Rosary

The Beast and the Lamb

The Feasts of Judaism

The Sacred Heart of Jesus

The Holy Spirit and Spiritual Gifts

Stewardship of the Earth

To check availability and publication dates, or for a description of each study, visit our website at www.twentythirdpublications.com or www.godswordtoday.com or call us at 1-800-321-0411.

Threshold Bible Study is available through your local bookstore or directly from the publisher. The following volume discounts are available from the publisher:

$12.95	(1-3 copies)
$11.95	(4-7 copies)
$10.95	(8-11 copies)
$9.95	(12 or more copies)